M.O.S.A.I.C.

Charleston, SC
www.PalmettoPublishing.com

M.O.S.A.I.C.:
Simplifying the Art of
Organizational Effectiveness and Change

First Edition

Hardcover ISBN: 978-1-68515-885-9
Paperback ISBN: 978-1-68515-886-6
eBook ISBN: 978-1-68515-887-3

Dedication

To those who have the courage
to speak the truth to power
for they can change the world

Table of Contents

Acknowledgments

I have had the good fortune to work with some incredibly skilled organizational effectiveness and change management professionals over the course of my career. My work and the content of this book has been influenced by them all. I wish to express a special thanks to Pat Cramer. Your wisdom and support were the catalyst for my career, and I wouldn't be where I am without you—your friendship is a gift I have always cherished. To Sandy Catalani, who tirelessly responded to any request for support regardless of how ridiculous it may have sounded at the time—your ability to see what I needed before I knew I needed it was never taken for granted. I'd like to particularly thank Vicki Poels, Paul Turner, Petra Schennach, and Michele Grisez who both read sections of the manuscript and contributed invaluable feedback. Vicki, your creative insights and support throughout this journey was invaluable—I am eternally grateful for your willingness to challenge my thinking and contribute to it. I'd also like to thank my many clients, both internal and external, who have prompted my thinking on these topics and challenged me to always view my work through the eyes of the client. Finally I would like to thank my wonderful husband of thirty-eight years, Bob, who has always served as a reliable sounding board and willing test subject. You are my rock—another thirty-eight years still wouldn't be enough time with you. My amazing sons, Mark and Jay, who have for years tolerated all the global travel that has made my work possible. Jay, your ability to bring fresh thinking to old concepts as we worked on this book was invaluable. To my parents, Kathleen and Jerry Durkin, who continue to watch over me. Thank you for giving me the confidence to venture into unfamiliar places—it serves me well in this field of work. I am deeply grateful to all of you.

Preface

Have you ever invested an exorbitant amount of time and energy on a project, believing that it needed to be perfect, only to see it fail? Early in my career, I was presenting to the senior vice president of marketing for a large financial organization. Five minutes into my presentation, I knew I was in trouble. All my carefully worded and politically correct slides describing the problem and possible solutions weren't hitting the mark. My boss, who had accompanied me to the meeting, moved her chair back, distancing herself from my imminent failure. My planned hour-long meeting was done in ten minutes. As we rode the crowded elevator from the executive suite back down to our departmental floor, she turned to me before exiting and said, "If you can't look an executive in the eye, tell him in simple language that he is about to screw up and have some practical ideas to keeping him from doing that, you don't belong in this business." I still remember the looks of pity from total strangers in that elevator. It was one of the most embarrassing but defining moments of my professional career.

That early and painful lesson taught me the value of simplicity. Whether it is diagnosing the problem, framing the conversation, or pinpointing the most critical inhibitors to success, you must keep it simple. Clients repeatedly tell me, "Your tools make it so simple. Can't you put it in a package for us?" This frequent request is the impetus for this book.

Why Should You Read This Book?

Organizational effectiveness (OE) is the measurement of how successfully an organization reaches its goals. There are hundreds of books and suggested processes available on OE and change management. Most of them fall into two categories. First there are those that focus primarily on the "softer" side of change, such as overcoming resistance and/or techniques that entice employees to adopt a change. Although these are important concepts to keep in mind, we have found that the most significant part of enticement is grounded in the organization's ability to quickly crystallize what needs to be accomplished and clearly outline the plan to accomplish it, yet that continues to be a challenge for many organizations. Then there are those publications that are theoretical in nature and/or focus solely on a single component of OE, such as strategy, organizational redesign, talent management, process improvement, culture, et cetera. These publications make important contributions because they explain the principles underlying the tools and practices recommended on the following pages, but are often presented with such complexity that it is paralyzing for those who are tasked with implementing change rather than studying it. *This book is different.* The MOSAIC change approach is not focused on the theory—it is all about the "what" and the "how."

MOSAIC provides an easy-to-use framework for identifying and resolving the most common internal obstacles that limit organizational effectiveness and impact the organization's ability to drive change. It is intended as a practical field guide. It is for the leader who does not have the luxury of having an OE professional on staff to help resolve and work on change issues, for the entrepreneur who needs some basic guidance on how to get a launch plan in place, and for the human resource leader or OE professional who is looking to expand their tool kit. My goal is to provide the reader with the same tools that I have successfully used as both an internal and external consultant.

How to Make the Most of This Book

There is only one chapter in this book that I encourage you to read fully. Chapter 1, "Introduction to the MOSAIC Change Framework," establishes the structure for the entire book. When people ask me how to think about OE work, this is the mental model I use. There are two significant elements of organizational effectiveness and change that are not reflected in traditional organizational models: the need for strong project management and the adherence to basic change management principles. Without these two elements, I can all but guarantee that your change efforts are likely to fail; therefore these are important parts of the MOSAIC change framework.

Having a conceptual understanding of each MOSAIC element and approaching the whole is how you can most effectively manage and integrate the parts of any change. This will also allow you to make the most use of each subsequent chapter and enable you to match the tools with specific problem areas in your own organization. The use of tools without a broader understanding of the organization as a system can prevent you from focusing on your root-cause problems, so *don't skip this chapter*!

Once you've read chapter 1, feel free to skip around from topic to topic. Devoting time and organizational energy to issues that are *nice to solve* but not *necessary to solve* is a common failure mode when managing organizational change, so look at the areas that seem to resonate with your observations about the challenges your organization faces, because solving the right problem is the first step toward a successful change effort. Finally, I'd encourage you to make this book a useful tool. Don't read it and put it on a shelf. Write in the margins and make it your own. Practice using the tools and adjust as necessary to make it work for you.

If you would like to download the MOSAIC change tools, get information on our workshops and training programs, are interested in participating in our MOSAIC online communities/forums, or are interested in becoming a MOSAIC certified change leader, you can find us online at www.mosaicchange.com.

Chapter 1

Introduction to the MOSAIC Change Framework

Every organization develops into its own unique piece of art over time. Some become beautiful creations that attract loyal customers, create dedicated employees and become the envy of the competition. Others turn out to be disappointing, with visible and unappealing flaws, unable to capture the attention of customers and with reputations that prevent them from attracting or retaining the talent required to grow and prosper. *Do you really know what it takes to ensure that your organization is in the first category?*

Whether your organization is large or small, publicly traded or privately held, a for-profit or a nonprofit or even a start-up, it is similar in one specific way—it is a system, a constantly changing organism comprised of multiple, interdependent parts: a mosaic. Each part functions as its own unique tile, but those tiles come together to form a pattern that ultimately defines your organization's shape and overall attractiveness.

There are basic tenets of working in mosaic art. The various tiles must fit perfectly together and be held in place with mortar or grout that serves as the glue to give the piece strength over time. Changing one tile without considering how it fits into the broader pattern can decrease the overall appeal of the final piece. Using a color that doesn't complement the broader pattern would be less pleasing to the eye and decrease the value of the final product. Organizations are no different. Like a mosaic, the various parts of your organization must complement one another. Making changes in one area without considering the impact on other parts of the organization can have unintended and costly implications. Failing to invest in the key elements of organizational "glue" will result in a loss of sustainability. At the end of the day, it all must align beautifully, or it loses its appeal, and it has less value. *The ability to understand and manage the interdependencies of the "tiles" in your organizational mosaic is essential to ensuring organizational effectiveness and change capability.*

My concern when I started this book was that it would make organizational effectiveness appear too simple. But honestly, most of the organizational problems that I am asked to solve are strikingly similar from client to client. I continue to encounter the same problems across vastly different types of organizations. These common challenges can paralyze the organization, causing leaders to invest excessive amounts of time on internal issues, which reduces time spent understanding their markets and serving their customers. The good news is that most of these problems are easily avoidable. By using the simple approach outlined in this book, you can resolve the most common internal organizational effectiveness issues.

Organizations and the landscape in which they operate can be complex, but the approach and tools that you use to drive improvements in your organization don't have to be. In over thirty years of working with clients, I continue to be reminded of Occam's razor, a problem-solving principle that states "the simplest solution is most likely the right one." Time after time this has proven to be the case with my clients. *Complexity kills most change efforts*, so change work needs to be practical, easy to use, and yield results quickly. In that spirit of simplicity, we developed the simple MOSAIC framework below as a standard way of thinking about how to approach organizational effectiveness and change in any type of organization. *Why do you need a framework?* Because just like mosaic art, each element of the framework must be considered if you want to successfully launch and (more importantly) sustain significant organizational change.

Let's look at each element of the MOSAIC change framework.

M.O.S.A.I.C. Change™ - Copyright 2022 © All Right Reserved

Mission

All organizational effectiveness and change management efforts start with a clear definition of what you are trying to accomplish. Be honest. How likely are you to jump on a bus if you have no idea where it is going? Why would your employees be any different? This statement of the end state you hope to achieve is critical to everything else you do, and it is the essence of a solid strategic plan. When we refer to "mission" as part of the MOSAIC change framework we are referring to not only your actual mission statement but also the strategic plan that helps you to accomplish that mission.

Many organizations underinvest time spent on strategy. Most will never take the time to fully evaluate their portfolio of product and service offerings, they won't take the time to do a robust competitive analysis, or engage in a host of other activities that could be helpful in creating a good strategic plan. However, most of them will benefit greatly from just engaging in a conversation about (1) their purpose (call it a vision or mission; it doesn't matter) and (2) the three to five "needle-mover" strategic outcomes that will enable them to achieve their mission. It doesn't have to be complex, and it doesn't have to take a four-day off-site meeting to complete. *Keep it simple.* For 80 percent of our clients, if you can get the right people in a room for less than a day, you can develop a solid strategic plan. The process for developing a simple "plan-on-a-page" can be found in chapter 2.

Organize

How you organize your people should always align with your strategy. What are you trying to accomplish? If your plan is to go to market by product line, you may choose to structure by product line. If you want to drive functional excellence, then you may choose to structure the organization along functional lines. If you want to expand to a certain geographic market, you may need to have staff on the ground in that part of the world. I believe that any structure can work if you have clarity on decision-making authority and the right rewards in place to drive collaborative behaviors. Reorganizing a business can cause unnecessary chaos and yield little for the disruption it causes. Leaders should be careful of pulling that lever unless there are critical reasons to do so. Before engaging in a restructuring, it is important to consider the alternatives suggested in this book, but if you are convinced that you need to reorganize, an approach to initiating an organizational redesign can be found in chapter 3.

Staff

Nothing happens in your organization without people. **People practices need to align with your strategy.** Do you have the right talent to produce today's products or services? Do you have the right talent to produce the products and services that you will need in the future? For example, if one of your key objectives is to develop software-based products, and 80 percent of your engineers are hardware experts, you are unlikely to accomplish your strategy. Are you hiring or developing the critical skills that you need to be and stay competitive? Do you know who your best employees are and do you know what it will take to retain them? Having the right leadership conversations about your workforce can lead you to better decisions in terms of how to most effectively manage your talent. Chapter 4 provides practical tools for evaluating the talent you need and developing the talent you already have.

Align

To sustain any change effort, the basic underpinnings of the organization must be set up to support the change. Replacing old habits with new habits creates the "stickiness" required to sustain change. That sounds simple, but it can be incredibly hard to execute. The power of the status quo is strong, and the pull to keep doing things the way they have always been done is perhaps the biggest challenge you will face in making meaningful change happen. Chapter 5 is all about addressing organizational "glue" and provides tools to ensure the key parts of your organization are aligned and the broader system is set up to support the changes you are implementing.

Implement

Change implementation requires good project management and a robust management operating system to stabilize the changes. Improvement ideas can be valuable, but not if your organization lacks the basic project management skills and/or discipline to implement those ideas. I've seen far too many changes fail because the organizations lacked a basic approach to managing the change project. The ability to define a clear scope of work, calculate the time that work will take, predict the cost of that work, anticipate and plan for potential risks, develop a solid communication plan, and ensure actions are well-executed are key to a successful change. Good project management demands a robust management operating system (MOS) to keep the organization informed about and connected to new expectations and new ways of operating. Chapter 6 outlines some basic project management tools to help you implement your change in a structured way.

Change Principles

Most change initiatives fail. Multiple studies have been done on the percentage of change projects that fail to deliver on the intended results with the average rate hovering around 70 percent. It isn't because people didn't work hard or didn't want to change. What I often find is that the plan is good and the leaders want the change to happen, but the organization is in violation of what I'll call the "five fatal flaws." These are the **five most common behavioral pitfalls that leaders must avoid when managing a change.** These rules are the underpinnings of a good change process; if you fail to abide by them, the likelihood of success is low. Make every effort to learn them and put them into practice, and they will be a force multiplier for your change efforts. These rules are outlined in chapter 7.

Summary

It is important to note that while change doesn't happen in a completely linear process, there is a clear order in which you should approach managing a change. Some steps must happen before others. For example, everything (and I mean *everything*) depends on your mission. Mission clarity is at the heart of what you are trying to do as an organization—it sets the strategic direction and defines your destination. Every other tile defines *how* you plan to arrive at that destination. How you organize your reporting structure is dependent on your mission. How you staff the organization is dependent on your mission. How should you align the rewards, policies, and processes? Well, that depends on your mission. And of course implementing a change is the ultimate "how" because it defines who needs to do what and when to fully execute the project plan. Working on any of the *hows* (O, S, A, I) before finalizing the *what* (M) is a waste of time and money. Get clear on your destination and then decide how to get there. The change principles are not part of the sequence. They are the muscles that leaders must exercise throughout the entire change process to execute and sustain the change. More about that in chapter 7.

Finally, although a good organizational diagnostic will identify them, the foundational elements of the MOSAIC framework intentionally do not focus on the plethora of external factors (e.g., changing market conditions, geopolitical issues, government regulations, customer issues) that can influence the success of your organization. MOSAIC focuses on eliminating the most common inhibitors to building the strong foundation of internal change capability required to respond to an ever-changing external environment. Once the MOSAIC change approach becomes habitual for your organization, you can minimize the need to look internally *down and in* and instead focus your attention *up and out* on your markets and customers.

Each of the MOSAIC elements is reviewed in detail in the chapters that follow.

Chapter 2

Clarify the Mission

Mission Is the "What" That Drives the "How"

Much has been published on the July 21, 1969, speech that John F. Kennedy gave to Congress regarding the importance of space exploration. The simple directive that the United States should "commit itself to achieving the goal, before this decade is out, of landing a man on the moon and returning him safely to Earth" provided a crisp end state that removed any ambiguity about the target to be achieved. To this day it remains one of the best examples of the mission clarity that I'm trying to illustrate. That simple statement was the catalyst for a well-executed plan that ultimately led to the moon landing. Simply put, *all change efforts start with a clear definition of what you are trying to accomplish.* Whether you are launching a specific initiative or a broad-scale organizational change, a clear definition of the desired end state is your starting point.

A strategic plan doesn't need to be complex. As a leader, don't underestimate the importance and power of setting a clear strategic direction for your organization. Having a simple one-page view of your strategic plan is the first step to realizing that plan. *It is important to note that when I say, "clarify your mission," I am referring to your entire strategic plan, not just your mission statement.* That plan should include your organization's mission, the three to five strategic outcomes you must achieve to accomplish that mission, the priority actions that will enable you to achieve those outcomes, and the most critical measures of your success, or key performance indicators (KPIs).

I've seen consultants who spend days arguing about the difference between a vision, mission, purpose, strategy, objective, goal, tactic, et cetera. Personally I find most of this a waste of time. As long as it results in a simple-to-communicate strategic plan, choose whatever terms work for your organization. Included on the following page is a template for a simple one-page plan. This plan-on-a-page (POP) is a simple method for developing a shared strategy for an individual, team, or organization.

The Plan-on-a-Page

Mission	Key Strategic Outcomes	Priority Actions		Owner	Due Date
		1a.			
		1b.			
	1. x	1c.			
		1d.			
x		1e.			
		2a.			
		2b.			
	2. x	2c.			
		2d.			
		2e.			
How We Measure Success | KPIs		3a.			
		3b.			
▪ x	3. x	3c.			
		3d.			
		3e.			
▪ x		4a.			
		4b.			
▪ x	4. x	4c.			
		4d.			
		4e.			
▪ x		5a.			
		5b.			
	5. x	5c.			
▪ x		5d.			
		5e.			

To illustrate the foundational MOSAIC concepts and tools, we'll use examples from a fictional company we'll refer to as the PAX-Z Golf Company. This will give you an opportunity to see how the MOSAIC tools can be applied within an organization to solve real problems. Let me introduce you to the PAX-Z Golf Company. PAX-Z:

- was established forty-two years ago in the midwestern part of the United States;

- provides a wide variety of golf equipment and golf apparel;

- has approximately 220 employees with an average tenure of more than twenty-plus years with the company; and

- is based predominantly in the United States but does have an office in Canada and a small sales office in Japan.

The PAX-Z executive team has recently realized that:

- their core business is declining (incoming recreational golfers are more tech savvy and expect better technology, but PAX-Z can't compete with the technology offered by its competition);

- they need a more technically savvy staff but have a hard time attracting younger talent; and

- they have a very broad portfolio for such a small company and are now struggling to deliver to their customers.

The PAX-Z executive team has decided to:

- shift from their current old-school approach and adopt more contemporary, technology-enabled processes;

- reduce the number of product offerings and shift from a broad-market approach to more of a niche-market appeal; and

- build a plan to become to be the premiere provider of golfing equipment for the recreational golfer.

A completed sample of the PAX-Z POP can be found on page 19, but let's look at each element of this simple planning tool and review the key steps for building your own simple POP.

Mission Statement

Think for a moment about the last time that you chose to invest your personal time on a work project. I don't mean when your boss told you to come in on a Saturday. I am talking about that feeling of real contribution that we all want to experience, when we know that what we are doing really matters. It has been said that people will work for a paycheck but die for a cause. When employees are aligned with the core purpose of the organization, all kinds of good things happen. They work harder. There is less conflict, because the strength of the commitment to a common purpose supersedes petty personal differences. And employees are less likely to leave your organization in search of more meaningful work, because they have already found it within your organization.

A mission or purpose statement should be simple enough to remember. And I mean *really* simple. It's a sentence, not a paragraph. It should serve as the aspirational rallying cry for the organization. A good mission statement is a single sentence that has three parts: We do what, for whom, and for what purpose?

I'm going to say this ten times in this book, but complexity kills! As a child I went to Catholic school. It was a formative experience and influences my approach to this day. I will always remember Sister Mary Leo saying, "If you don't have the concept simple and clear in your own mind, how can you communicate it to others simply and clearly?" She was right. Avoid the desire to load up your purpose statement with a list of your strategic outcomes—adding unnecessary words distracts from what you are trying to communicate.

If you are the kind of person who just wants to understand the concept, jump to the next chapter. If you want to explore a more detailed process for building a mission statement, that information is included on the following page.

Building a Mission Statement

Here is how to develop a simple and clear mission statement:

1. Grab a piece of paper and make three columns:

We do *what?*	For *whom?*	For *what purpose?*

2. Jot down your thoughts for each column. You can do this by yourself or, if you are working with a team, have everyone do it.

3. If you are working with a team, pull together the input for each column and agree on each of the three parts.

4. Engage in a conversation to be sure that you have clarified…

   a. …what you really do? (This decision can either expand or narrow your focus. The strategic decisions you make if you identify yourself as "boat builders" could be quite different than if you view yourself as an organization that "enables water travel.")

   b. …who you do it for? (This generally leads to a good discussion of who you really plan to serve. Shareholders? Customers? A specific market segment? The general public?) Again, this decision will influence the strategic choices you make, so be clear about it.

   c. …why you do it? (To drive profit? To ensure a return to stakeholders? To protect public health? To promote freedom?) There isn't a wrong answer here. But of all three parts of the question, this is the one that will hook employees. If they value why you are doing what you are doing, they are more likely to see themselves as part of your overall mission.

5. Finally, pull the answers to each of the columns together to create one crisp statement that is easy for your employees to remember. Don't spend a lot of time wordsmithing. You can make it perfect later. Just get the essence of it and move on. Remember: keep it simple! Once you get it defined, document your mission on your POP.

Let's look at our PAX-Z Golf Company example. When the executive leadership team got together, their brainstorm session on their mission statement yielded the following input:

Mission/Purpose Statement: Pax-Z Golf Company Brainstorm

We do *what?*	For *whom?*	For *what purpose?*
• Produce golf clubs and apparel for amateur golfers • Offer innovative golf equipment for golfers • Build affordable but customized clubs and golfing products • Provide clothing and clubs for golfers • Equip golfers for their game • Make golf fun for everyone	• Golfers • Amateur golfers • Golfer wannabes • Discerning golfers • All golfers • Golfers • New golfers	• To make a profit for PAX-Z • To offer something unique but affordable to golfers • To issue a return to shareholders • To enhance the industry • To become the leading producer of golf clubs and apparel • To deliver high-performance golf stuff

After a robust discussion, the leadership team adopted the following statement as the mission for the PAX-Z Golf Company:

Mission

Build affordable, semi-customized clubs and golfing products for recreational golfers to broaden golf's appeal to a wider audience

It is important to note that the conversation is perhaps the most valuable part of the activity. By investing thirty-five minutes in this simple exercise, the team was able to discuss their various perspectives, surface disconnects, and ultimately align on one common purpose for the organization. This step is essential before you move forward to identify the most critical strategic outcomes that must be achieved to accomplish your mission.

Strategic Outcomes

Have you ever played Kim's game? It was derived from Rudyard Kipling's 1901 novel in which the game is played as part of the protagonist's training as a spy. Someone shows you a tray with twenty objects, takes it away, and then asks you to remember as many items as you can that were on the tray. To this day it continues to be used to improve one's observational abilities. Like most people, I was always terrible at that game, but it has continued to remind me of the importance of focus.

In 1956, George Miller, a cognitive psychologist from Harvard University's Department of Psychology, conducted research on information theory. As a result of his research, he published one of the most influential papers in psychology and established what came to be known as Miller's rule of seven. Through his research, he found that the average person is severely limited in terms of the amount of information they can receive, process, and remember and that short-term memory can hold seven (plus or minus two) items because it only has a certain number of "slots" in which items can be stored. Basically it means that people can remember and focus on only a handful of things at the same time—five on the low side and nine for the brightest of us. Miller's study was focused on short-term memory and the ability to retain knowledge of digits, words, or chess positions, but his research is quite relevant to the topic of organizational change. When considering an employee's ability to retain and execute key bodies of work, we must adopt Miller's theory. Similar to Kim's game, we have found that most employees can retain and successfully execute no more than three to five key bodies of work. Therefore we have adopted three to five as the realistic target for most organizations when planning your strategic outcomes.

I have yet to meet an organization that had unlimited resources, yet I continually see clients bury the organization in one initiative after another: a clear violation of Miller's rule of seven. When you focus your limited resources on what matters most, you need to clearly define and continually communicate the key strategic outcomes the organization must achieve. In the absence of a clear strategy that outlines the priority work to be done, day-to-day decision-making is driven by what employees *assume* is most critical. This diverts valuable organizational capacity away from what really matters. Therefore it is critically important to focus all your employees' energy on your three to five "needle movers." These should be the most critical outcomes your organization needs to accomplish to fulfill your mission. Strategic outcomes should be focused on *what* you need to accomplish, not *how* you plan to accomplish it.

Your mission and strategic outcomes serve as the backdrop for all organizational planning. The simple truth is that if you don't have a clear definition of WHAT you are trying to accomplish (that is well understood by those who need to accomplish it), then I can guarantee that you are wasting time and money. When employees aren't completely aligned on the mission and don't have a common understanding of the key strategic priorities, they unconsciously start to work at cross-purposes. In most organizations, if you ask twenty employees to define the five most critical strategic outcomes required to accomplish the mission, you'll get significantly different answers. This is a common and costly problem. For example, if Doris thinks outcomes A, B, and C are the most important needle movers, and Neal thinks X, Y, and Z are, they line up their daily work to accomplish what they think is most important to be done. When Doris observes Neal working on what she perceives to be less critical work, she begins to question Neal's contribution. Her thoughts become, "What is he doing? Why would he waste his time on that?" or "Why doesn't Neal get it?" The absence of a simple, shared understanding of the plan begins to erode relationships across the team. Unfortunately this situation often results in an inaccurate definition of the problem to be solved. Leaders will request team building when the real problem is simply a lack of clarity and alignment on work priorities.

To develop your strategic outcomes:

1. Pick a time frame for accomplishing your purpose. Are you developing a plan that should be executed in one year? Eighteen months? Three years? Markets change quickly. There is no right answer. Most of my clients have shifted from longer-term planning (five to seven years) to no more than three. And most of the start-ups I work with don't look beyond the next year. If you do decide to select a longer-term planning horizon, you'll need to set clear milestones to monitor your performance. Let's assume that we select a three-year time horizon for the plan.

2. Ask yourself, "Three years from now, what are the three to five most important outcomes that we must achieve in order to accomplish our mission/purpose?"

   REMINDER: focus on outcomes, not actions. For example, "robust marketing and brand strategy" is an outcome, but "establish partnerships with schools and golf courses to expand awareness" is an action to be taken to achieve that outcome. The first one defines *what* you need to accomplish; the second is one part of a larger plan for *how* you will do it.

3. Finalize the most critical strategic priorities and put them on your POP.

As you can see in the example on the following page, after developing their mission statement, the PAX-Z executive team defined four strategic outcomes that needed to be achieved to execute their mission. They did a good job of not responding to the need to 'fill the page'. Instead they intentionally selected four, not five, strategic outcomes. This was good. If you can accomplish your mission| purpose with less than five key strategic outcomes, then do it.

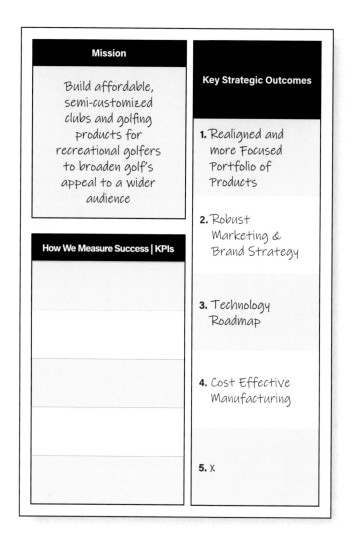

Priority Actions

Once you've developed your strategic priorities, you'll need to identify the actions that must be taken to accomplish each strategic outcome. While the strategic outcome is the "what," priority actions represent the "how." Priority actions <u>always start with a verb</u>. Again, remember Miller's rule of seven. Don't list *every* action that could be taken. Identify the *most critical* actions to be taken.

This is how to develop your priority actions:

1. For each strategic outcome, ask yourself, "What are the most important actions we should take to ensure that the strategic outcomes we need are achieved?" After you brainstorm, make sure to separate all the actions that are *nice to have* from the few actions that are *must-haves,* and then align on the priority actions.

2. For each agreed upon action, assign one person to lead the action to closure. This is often referred to in program management as the one-belly-button rule. This person may involve others in getting the work done, but as the leader, you need one individual to own the responsibility for ensuring that the work is completed.

3. Assign a tentative completion date to each action. You'll find more about the importance of this when we cover implementation in chapter 6.

REMEMBER: The goal is to create a plan for *focused action.* Some things to avoid when building priority actions:

*   *Not including the correct verb with each action.* There is a huge difference between "develop a plan" and "execute the plan." It could take you an hour to develop a plan but take years to execute it. *Verbs matter!* Clarity on the action will define how long it takes and who should do it, so always include a verb with your defined actions.

*   It is also worth noting that passive verbs such as "participate" or "facilitate" should be avoided. Many functional groups (HR, finance, IT, etc.) tend to build plans with passive verbs, which creates the appearance that functions are mere bystanders rather than actively engaged in accomplishing the plan. As a person who has been in a functional support role for most of my career, I always wanted to be seen as in the game rather than on the sidelines, so if your name is on the plan, have active, not passive, verbs as part of your assigned actions.

*   *The tendency to just list all the current work underway.* It is best to start with a clean sheet of paper. Ask the team, "If we had to choose from this day forward, what are the most important actions to be taken?" Of course additional subtasks will be required to fully achieve the strategic outcome, but this will get the team focused on the most critical actions and hopefully eliminate activity that is currently underway but should be stopped in favor of more meaningful actions.

*   *Assigning multiple owners to an action.* If you feel the need to list everyone who wants to be involved in that action, you can, but each action should have one clear owner who is responsible for working with others to complete the action.

*   *Frontloading all the due dates.* Often teams get excited about having a concrete plan, and they want to execute quickly. However, it is better to establish a realistic schedule to avoid having the team become demotivated when they can't get their actions across the finish line by the defined due dates.

As illustrated below, PAX-Z agreed on the priority actions for each of their four key strategic outcomes. Again, avoid the need to fill the page. If you can achieve the strategic outcome with fewer actions, then attempt to do so.

Key Strategic Outcomes	Priority Actions
1. Realigned and more Focused Portfolio of Products	**1a.** Assess current portfolio of products and make keep/exit recommendations to Executive Leadership Team.
	1b. Based on approved recommendations (1a), develop project plan to ensure execution by end of year.
	1c. Develop an external communication strategy to ensure that partners, customers, vendors, etc. are aware of changes to our product offerings.
	1d. Ensure that manufacturing has changed production processes to align with leadership decisions regarding product offerings.
	1e.
2. Robust Marketing and Brand Strategy	**2a.** Hire external vendor to conduct a market assessment to define key needs/wants of the Recreational Market Segment.
	2b. Revise our 'brand' identity to appeal to the Recreational Market Segment.
	2c. Establish partnerships with schools/golf courses/etc. to expand awareness.
	2d. Develop a marketing campaign (including key golf expos) to 'reintroduce' the new PAX-Z to the market.
	2e. Work with Marketing VP to assess and determine talent requirements for the Marketing Team.
3. Technology Roadmap	**3a.** Partner with Marketing to complete a competitive assessment to better understand the technical capabilities of our competition.
	3b. Identify key technology 'needle movers' for PAX-Z and associated investment costs.
	3c. Recruit 2-3 engineers with backgrounds in AI engineering, computer science, & physics. Golf experience preferred.
	3d. Build a 3-year technology roadmap to illustrate the availability of new product offerings and associated investment timing.
	3e.
4. Cost-effective Manufacturing	**4a.** Evaluate current manufacturing locations and cost - Make recommendations on how to centralize manufacturing to shorten delivery times, reduce footprint and overall cost.
	4b. Complete an assessment of our current supply chain (raw materials availability, supplier quality, etc.) and make recommended changes to improve overall quality and drive cost reduction.
	4c. Based on final senior leadership team recommendations, develop final project plan.
	4d. Based on final approvals define and document new manufacturing and supply chain processes.
	4e.

Success Metrics | Key Performance Indicators (KPIs)

It is difficult to measure the success of your strategic plan if you don't know what defines success. By identifying and measuring a few key performance indicators (KPIs), you will be able to measure your progress. To develop KPIs, ask, *"What are the critical few measures that we will use to define successful completion of the plan?"* Keep in mind that you must build a system of measurement for every KPI. It can take a significant amount of time to gather and report KPI data, especially if you don't have access to automated systems that make it easy to do so. So again, keep it simple! Select no more than three to five specific, measurable, well-written KPIs, and then take the time necessary to build a process to measure and report on each one.

Although they could have selected several other options, PAX-Z decided to only measure the four Success Metrics | KPIs that you see below.

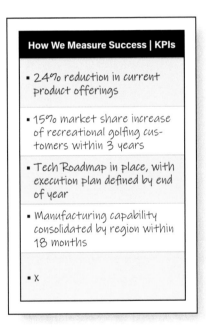

How We Measure Success | KPIs

- 24% reduction in current product offerings

- 15% market share increase of recreational golfing customers within 3 years

- Tech Roadmap in place, with execution plan defined by end of year

- Manufacturing capability consolidated by region within 18 months

- X

Summary

So based on this chapter, here are the common pitfalls to avoid in the "M" or MISSION component of the MOSAIC framework:

- Building an action plan in the absence of a clear mission and strategy (REMEMBER—The "what" needs to be clear before you define the "how"!)

- The inability to narrow the focus for the organization to the most critical needle-mover work (this applies both to the number of strategic outcomes and the number of priority actions)

- Too many success metrics | KPIs, which diverts energy into measuring and monitoring and away from work that truly supports your customers

- Investing time during the planning session "working the plan" instead of "planning the plan" (once the plan is in place, then you can work the plan)

Can you build something more complex than the POP described above? Absolutely. I have seen strategic plans that exceed 130 pages in length. Months of staff time are literally spent in research and analysis to inform that level of planning. A multitude of high-quality firms exist to support leaders with this effort, and it can provide valuable insights into your competitors, markets, et cetera. And while there is value in those insights, 90 percent of the clients I have had the opportunity to work with have neither the money nor the time to engage in that level of planning. And unfortunately many that do will want to justify the spending by ending up with something complex and often difficult to translate into an executable plan. Engaging in conversations about your competition, your go-to-market strategy, et cetera is always helpful but with most clients, I've found that if you pull together some of your most experienced and talented employees and follow the POP guidance outlined above, in less than a day, you can develop a basic strategic plan for your organization.

Okay, so now you have a plan that defines what you want to accomplish. It's a great start, but a plan has little value if you can't execute that plan. Let's look at the other elements of MOSAIC that are all about the "how."

* * *

The Foundational Tool: Plan-on-a-Page

SAMPLE: Final PAX-Z Golf Company Plan-on-a-Page

The Plan-on-a-Page for: PAX-Z Golf Company

Mission	Key Strategic Outcomes	Priority Actions	Owner	Due Date
Build affordable, semicustomized clubs and golfing products for recreational golfers to broaden golf's appeal to a wider audience.	1. Realigned and more Focused Portfolio of Products	**1a.** Assess current portfolio of products and make keep/exit recommendations to executive leadership team.	Doris	Feb 17
		1b. Based on approved recommendations (1a), develop project plan to ensure execution by end of year.	Doris/Gert	March 13
		1c. Develop an external communication strategy to ensure that partners, customers, vendors, et cetera are aware of changes to our product offerings.	Doris/Neal	April 30
		1d. Ensure that manufacturing has changed production processes to align with leadership decisions regarding product offerings.	Fred	May 5
		1e.		
How We Measure Success | KPIs	2. Robust Marketing and Brand Strategy	**2a.** Hire external vendor to conduct a market assessment to define key needs/wants of the recreational market segment.	Doris	Jan 11
		2b. Revise our brand identity to appeal to the recreational market segment.	Doris/Sam	April 3
• 24 percent reduction in current product offerings		**2c.** Establish partnerships with schools and golf courses to expand awareness.	Neal/Marsha	June 3
		2d. Develop a marketing campaign (including key golf expos) to reintroduce the new PAX-Z to the market.	Doris/Sam	April 16
		2e. Work with marketing VP to assess and determine talent requirements for the marketing team.	Doris/**Maggie**	Feb 1
• 15 percent market-share increase in recreational golfing customers within three years	3. Technology Roadmap	**3a.** Partner with marketing to complete a competitive assessment to better understand the technical capabilities of our competition.	Vicki	Feb 9
		3b. Identify key technology needle movers for PAX-Z and associated investment costs.	Vicki/Kan	Apr 1
		3c. Recruit two to three engineers with backgrounds in AI engineering, computer science, and physics. Golf experience preferred.	Vicki/**Maggie**	June 4
		3d. Build a three-year technology roadmap to illustrate the availability of new product offerings and associated investment timing.	Vicki/Hugh	July 13
• Tech roadmap in place with execution plan defined by end of year		**3e.**		
	4. Cost-effective Manufacturing	**4a.** Evaluate current manufacturing locations and cost. Make recommendations on how to centralize manufacturing to shorten delivery times and reduce footprint and overall cost.	Fred	April 2
		4b. Complete an assessment of our current supply chain (raw materials availability, supplier quality, etc.) and make recommended changes to improve overall quality and drive cost reduction.	Fred/**Laura**	May 7
		4c. Based on final senior leadership team recommendations, develop final project plan.	Fred	July 10
• Manufacturing capability consolidated by region within eighteen months		**4d.** Based on final approvals, define and document new manufacturing and supply chain processes.	Fred/Tommy	Sept 1
		4e.		
		5a.		
		5b.		
		5c.		
		5d.		
		5e.		

Chapter 3

Organize to Support the Mission

Choosing to reorganize as the first solution to a problem is a terrible idea!

For years clients have called me to get assistance in restructuring their organizations. Most often the calls come from a leader who has stepped into a new role, has observed high levels of dysfunction, and incorrectly assumes that changing the organization structure will resolve that dysfunction. Of course nothing grabs the attention of the organization more than a change in reporting relationships. However, restructuring an organization can wreak havoc, causing significant disruption and unrest among the troops if not executed with clarity and intent. If done well, it will send a clear message about what is important, it will focus your people on the mission, and it will facilitate efficient and effective interactions throughout the organization. If done poorly, you will have distracted the organization, lost credibility as a leader, and probably wasted a lot of time and money. So leaders should be *very* selective about if, when, and how often they reorganize.

In my experience, almost any organization structure can work if roles and responsibilities are clearly defined and the right levels of accountability are in place to ensure collaboration across organizational boundaries. The primary reason to undertake the challenge of redesigning an organization is if your current structure fails to align with your strategy. For example, if your current structure hampers your ability to scale the organization for growth, then you may want to consider a reorganization. The basic rule I suggest my clients follow is to avoid restructuring your organization unless you have made significant shifts in your strategy that require you to do so.

Often what people label as an organization-structure problem is not solved by reorganizing. Here are two options to consider before you undertake a restructuring project.

First, clarify roles and responsibilities and ensure clear decision-making authority. Ask yourself these questions:

- Are roles and responsibilities clearly defined in our current organization (i.e., employees clearly understand who is supposed to do what)?

- Is it clear who has the authority to make decisions for key bodies of work?

If the answer to these two questions is 'no', you may not need to restructure the organization. Instead invest the time necessary to clarify what I call "Who has the X?"

Who Has the X?

Most businesspeople are familiar with the RASCI model. It is a commonly used program-management tool developed in the 1950s that is used to clarify roles and responsibilities within an organization. It is basically a matrix that identifies roles across the horizontal and the tasks and/or decisions to be made across the vertical. Then you assign roles to each task using the following designations:

- Who is responsible? (R)
- Who is accountable to sign off on the final project? (A)
- Who will support the completion of the task? (S)
- Who should be consulted? (C)
- Who should be informed but not necessarily consulted? (I)

Early in my career, I facilitated a variety of RASCI sessions. Most of the time, it was a huge waste of time. Teams argued for hours about their level of involvement, and when we finally finished documenting the input, it ended up on a shelf, and no one ever looked at it again. After multiple frustrating meetings, I realized the RASCI discussion was really about who was in charge and who had the power to make the decisions. The other designations made people feel like they had some role but weren't material to how work actually happened. So I shifted gears. I started using the simple tool below. This is a sample from the PAX-Z leadership team.

Who Has the X? PAX-Z Executive Team

KEY TASK AND/OR DECISION	CEO (Sam)	Manufacturing (Fred)	Commercial & Retail (Neal)	Strategy & Marketing (Doris)	Engineering & Technology (Vicki)	Human Resources (Maggie)	Finance (Claudio)
Establish annual revenue targets	X						
Final approval on new business opportunities	X						
Set the sales approach for new business opportunities			X				
Review and approve new brand identity				X			
Finalize product offerings catalogue				X			
Develop marketing campaigns				X			
Finalize the annual operating plan budget							X
Finalize IT investment decisions/timing					X		
Develop strategic talent management approach						X	
Final recommendations on MFG centralization		X					

Completing the "Who Has the X?" Tool

Here is a simple process for facilitating the "Who Has the X?" conversation:

1. Across the horizontal part of the chart, list all the roles that could take on the work. As you can see from the PAX-Z example on the prior page, each member of the CEO's executive team is listed across the top part of the chart.

2. Down the vertical side of the chart, make a list of the most controversial bodies of work. Do not list all the work that is happening or every decision that needs to be made. Focus on tasks where there is duplication of effort (multiple people trying to control the same work) or confusion over who has the final authority for that work. Make sure that each task starts with a verb! This will help you differentiate different parts of the same area of work.

3. Review what it means to "have the X." If you have the X, you lead. You put in the effort to ensure input from the right people *before* you decide. And when push comes to shove, you get 51 percent of the vote in terms of decision-making authority.

4. Explain what it does not mean to have the X. It does not mean that you can make unilateral decisions without input from key stakeholders.

5. Explain the importance of having only one X in each row. The whole point of the exercise is to clarify the primary task and/or decision owner, so there should be only one X for each task and/or decision area.

The most important part of the "Who has the X?" process is the conversation and final agreement on how work will happen and how final decisions will be made. For example, PAX-Z Golf is a rather small company, but as they had grown, work had been moved to whoever was available at the time rather than leaders assigning that work to the place it probably belonged. For example, in the early days of PAX-Z, the business leaders did everything because they didn't have the luxury of having functional support staff. Neal, as the head of the commercial and retail business, had always been the final decision maker on the brand for his business because there weren't any professional marketing resources available to him. When Sam, the CEO, hired Doris Chen as the head of strategy and marketing, she felt that branding was her responsibility. As a result of the "Who has the X?" discussion, Neal and Doris had a chance to discuss how they could work together, but they were also able to clarify that Neal would have significant input but Doris would lead the effort and have the 51 percent of the vote when deciding on the overall branding strategy for PAX-Z, which provided much needed clarity.

Building Service Level Agreements

The second option to try before restructuring your organization is to develop internal service-level agreements (SLAs).

Leaders often want to reorganize because they want to gain control over a part of the organization that fails to meet their expectations. This was not an issue within PAX-Z, so let's step away from PAX-Z for a moment, and I'll give you a different example that better illustrates the issue.

Mary oversees corporate sales for her organization. Each month she is responsible for pulling all the financial information on that month's sales (revenue, sales pipeline, status of key accounts, etc.) and sending a report to the CEO. To pull accurate results, she needs all the sales information put into the computer system by the first of each month. The business units each manage their own sales teams, so these resources perform sales-related activities, but they don't work for Mary; they work for the business leads. As a result, the sales teams don't want to spend any time doing data input, because they don't need that data to do their jobs. However, Mary is unable to do her job if they don't provide the input. It stands to reason that one way Mary can solve her problem is to have authority over all the sales resources, which is why she has been pushing the CEO to move all the sales-related resources to work for her. Could the CEO restructure? Sure. Or he could consider investing time to develop an SLA between Mary and the business unit leaders.

SLAs are commonly used with external vendors, but they can be equally as effective inside your organization. An SLA is an agreement that is used to maintain a level of service between departments. It is a document that identifies specific performance-level expectations that one work unit has from another work unit. Internal service-level agreements are not about products or services. An SLA focuses on issues such as timeliness, quality, cost, or behaviors that you need from others to accomplish your work. SLAs are designed to drive collaborative behaviors and actions that ensure a shared responsibility for success across the broader organization.

To successfully develop an SLA, all parties need to reach a mutual understanding. Through the process, each side learns what is most important to the other party before moving forward. The process often begins with each party drafting its own best-case SLA, which defines the ideal or preferred outcome, what it believes it has to offer to the other parties, and what points may be nonnegotiable on its side. This is each party's starting position for the discussion.

A sample SLA for Mary's situation is shown on the following page.

Internal Service-Level Agreement for *Corporate Sales*

FACTOR	SPECIFIC REQUEST	WHAT IS THE TARGET?	HOW IT WILL BE MEASURED
QUALITY	• All sales roles across the company will use Salesforce (not Excel reports) to document targets in the sales pipeline. • All information on sales targets will be completely filled out in Salesforce per agreed-upon "must-have" data fields.	100 percent 95 percent	Quarterly Salesforce usage report
TIMELINESS	• All sales staff will input all financial data into Salesforce by close of business on the first Monday of each month. • Legal will provide a response to (approve or reject) all sales bids within forty-eight hours of submission to ensure timely response to customers.	95 percent 95 percent	Sales financial report Executive team review meeting discussion
COST	• Business-unit sales campaigns will not exceed 2 percent of campaign budget preapproved by corporate sales. • Recruiting costs for all new sales staff will be agreed to with the business leader prior to posting the job.	<2 percent variance across all campaigns 100 percent agreement	Quarterly budget report Executive team review meeting discussion
BEHAVIORS	• Business-unit sales leader will include corporate sales office in all quarterly meetings with our top-tier accounts. • Business-unit talent reviews will include feedback on business-unit sales roles from corporate sales.	100 percent 100 percent	Exceptions reviewed at quarterly sales offsite

Mary's SLA reflects her agreements with multiple groups, including:

- Business units to ensure that she receives the right level of sales data input so she can accurately complete her sales reports for the CEO,

- Human Resources to ensure staffing costs for sales are well controlled, and

- Legal to ensure sales bid approvals don't take too long.

As you can see in this example, some items are essential negotiating points but difficult to measure. For example, under expected behaviors, Mary doesn't want corporate sales to be excluded from sales meetings that the business units set up with the company's largest accounts. To understand how to manage sales across the company (not just by business unit), she wants to be sure that she is invited to attend those meetings. Spending a lot of time documenting meeting attendance and building reports in order to measure adherence to that SLA item is probably overkill. The easiest way to measure if the right behavior is happening is to put it on the leadership staff meeting as a checkpoint for discussion. Is it happening? Isn't it? Why? Establishing ongoing reviews of whether people are adhering to the agreements is a good way to ensure they happen. In chapter 6 we'll talk more about the importance of a good management operating system and a strong meeting cadence.

Here is how to develop internal service-level agreements:

1. Distribute the template and ask both parties to document what they need from each other. They should be clear and specific regarding their expectations in terms of timeliness, cost, quality, or better behaviors. Each request should have a clearly defined metric. If it isn't written in a way that it can be measured, you won't be able to tell if it was ever achieved, so ensure the requests are specific! Replace a request such as "Sales staff will input data" with something like "Sales staff will input all financial data by close of business on the first Monday of each month."

2. Set up a meeting with both parties present to review the input and conduct an item-by-item review of all requests. Emphasize that this is an initial agreement that will be put in place and then reviewed to ensure the metrics are appropriate. Mediate the discussion until both parties are aligned and agree to abide by the SLA.

3. Discuss and agree on how you plan to implement the final agreement:

   a. Who will need to change their current work to ensure compliance with the new agreement?

   b. How will you communicate the SLA to ensure all parties understand the agreements and new expectations?

3. Agree to (and set up) a schedule of meetings to ensure a regular review of the agreement. How often will we meet to review adherence? Who will set up the review meetings? Then discuss: Are both parties living up to the agreement? Should changes be made to improve either party's ability to fulfill the agreement? Then make modifications as indicated.

SLAs can take several review cycles to fully implement, so don't give up too quickly on the SLA process. Mature organizations that are effective at collaboration across boundaries will implement quickly, but it may take more time for less mature organizations, so give it some time before you jump to restructuring.

A Basic Approach to Restructuring Your Organization

In most cases a lack of clear decision-making authority and/or the ability to gain control over other parts of the organization is behind most requests to reorganize, so please try the two items above before undertaking a restructuring.

As I mentioned earlier, if not managed well, an organizational redesign can cause significant disruption. Based on that, I debated if I should include anything at all in terms of guidance on how to approach a basic organizational redesign. Finally I acknowledged that most leaders are going to do it anyway, often without any guidance at all. So if you have concluded that your only choice is to restructure, and you have the capability (appropriate level of competence and implementation support) to do it, I have outlined below a standard approach to conducting an organizational redesign.

To arrive at the best structural solution, it is important that you follow each step outlined below. Again, seek professional help if you are not familiar with leading an organizational redesign process.

1. Establish clear organization design criteria. Most clients jump right in and start drawing organizational charts. Please don't! If you don't define the criteria by which you will ultimately choose an organizational structure, the choice tends to be based on limited considerations and/or the loudest voice in the room. Effective organization (structure) design criteria:

    a. defines the structural elements required to accomplish the strategic plan;

    b. identifies measurable and observable outcomes (not structural options); and

    c. enables you to differentiate between structural options.

    Examples of good structural design criteria are shown below.

SAMPLE: Organization Design Criteria

Our Ideal Organizational Structure Will

- improve our ability to serve our customers;
- reduce our recurring cost by no less than 12 percent ($1.3 million in annual savings);
- strengthen our regional sales efforts in new markets;
- simplify reporting relationships to eliminate ambiguity and improve accountability;
- eliminate "shadow" work by ensuring all functional work resides within the functions (finance, HR, IT, marketing, etc.);
- improve our ability to integrate acquisitions effectively; and
- help us to streamline our key processes to standardize work, which enables us to scale/grow.

2. <u>Pull together a design-planning team.</u> These should be some of your best thought leaders. An ideal design-planning team is comprised of:

   a. a wide cross-section of the organization that represents business units, functions, and geographies (leaving stakeholder groups out of the planning process limits buy-in and creates risk in the quality of the final plan, so when in doubt, expand the group);

   b. high-potential talent that recognizes and wants to participate in developing a structure that can overcome today's challenges and prepare the organization for future challenges (those who will have to live with the decisions made and seasoned experts who can balance the opportunities with the potential risks);

   c. individuals who are viewed as credible by the organization (we want the broader organization to be able to say, "The team that made the recommendations adequately represented my business/function/region/etc.");

   d. individuals who are viewed as credible by the executive leadership team (we want the leadership team to be able to say, "If I wasn't invited, at least I trust the person who was…");

   e. a balance of those who are critical and must return to their day jobs after the planning session, and those who could potentially serve as part of an ongoing implementation team if needed; and

   f. individuals who are able to have an open, unimpeded dialogue about the current organization without feeling at risk of doing so based on who is in the room.

When identifying the design team, consider using the following criteria.

SAMPLE: Design Team Selection Criteria

The Ideal Participant Will

- not be wedded to your current structure, so they can think openly about new possibilities;
- have no personal interest in the outcome and won't design themselves a seat at the table to serve their personal interest;
- display conversational courage and be willing to challenge the status quo and speak up on current challenges that could be positively impacted by structural changes;
- be able to rise above their current role to see the possibilities ("We could improve X if...");
- be able to adequately represent their business, function, and geography and speak to the positive or negative impact of potential changes in structure; and
- have depth/breadth of knowledge of how the organization operates (they know the risks of change and can help build a plan to mitigate those risks).

3. <u>Assemble the design planning team and facilitate them through the following conversation.</u>

   a. Have the executive sponsor of the potential restructuring effort kick off the meeting with an overview of why leadership is exploring a restructure and a quick review of the structural design criteria.

   b. Establish any necessary ground rules about the meeting. Sample ground rules are listed below.

SAMPLE: Design Team Meeting Ground Rules

Design Team Meeting Ground Rules

- This is an exploratory meeting, so keep this discussion confidential!
- Think big and be open to new possibilities for how to structure.
- No names in boxes, no names in discussions—this is about the structure, not the people in the structure.
- Drive for consensus—we have reached consensus when we can say things like this:
    - "It may not be my idea, but when I leave this room, I will support it as if it were."
    - "It may not be the best result for me, but it is the best result for our company."
- Consensus does not imply that majority rules / absolute agreement / it was the perfect solution / the highest-level participant decided.
- There should be only one conversation unless in group work.
- There should be equal participation.
- Leave your title at the door and share the airspace.

   c. Have a short, open discussion about what is working well today that should be maintained in any future structure, and discuss what isn't working and why that could be improved in a future structure. This will encourage the open brainstorming you need displayed throughout the process.

EXERCISE: Developing Structural Options

What is **WORKING WELL** in our current structure?	What **DOESN'T WORK** about our current structure that could be improved?

d. Establish working teams comprised of a wide variety of cross-functional participants. Mix it up to ensure they challenge one another. The number of teams will vary depending on how many participants are in the group, but don't have any fewer than three teams. Ask each team to develop a structural proposal that includes an organization chart and a list of the advantages and disadvantages associated with adopting the proposed structure. The sample below illustrates one option submitted by a team for how to restructure PAX-Z at the executive level to meet the organization design criteria. **Remind them not to put any names on charts and not to use any names in discussions!**

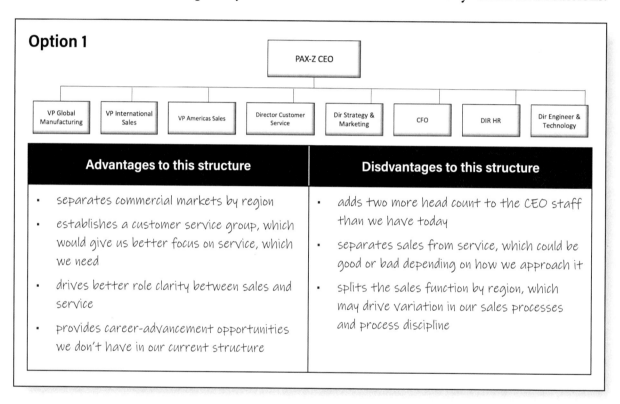

e. Bring the whole team back together and have each team discuss their proposed structure. Compare each option to the original design criteria in the illustration on the following page. Which one checks most of the boxes? As you can see, option 1 appears to be the best choice since it meets five of the design criteria elements, and the other two options only meet four each. Once you have identified the organization that best fits your organization design criteria, pull in any elements of the other options that you would like to incorporate, and finalize your proposed design. Validate that the team is committed to the final recommendation and will jointly "own" the final outcome when presenting the final recommendation to the leadership team.

Comparing Options

Design Criteria	Option 1	Option 2	Option 3
improves our ability to serve our customers	✓	✓	✓
reduces our recurring cost by no less than 12 percent ($1.3 million in annual savings)			✓
strengthens our regional sales efforts in new markets	✓	✓	✓
simplifies reporting relationships to eliminate ambiguity and improve accountability	✓		
eliminates "shadow" work by ensuring all functional work resides within the functions (finance, HR, IT, marketing, etc.)	✓	✓	✓
improves our ability to integrate acquisitions effectively	✓		
helps us to streamline our key processes to standardize work, which enables us to scale/grow		✓	

f. Bring in the executive sponsor and have the design-planning team review their proposed structure in detail. It is important to recognize that there is *no such thing as a perfect structure*. Every structure brings trade-offs. A leader must pick the best structure to execute the mission, define the risks associated with that structure, and then mitigate those risks most effectively.

g. If you decide to implement your structure, ask the design planning team to complete the simple risk assessment template that can be found in chapter 6 along with other implementation tools.

Summary

So based on this chapter, here are the common pitfalls to avoid in the "O" or ORGANIZE component of the MOSAIC framework:

- attempting to reorganize when organizational structure is not the real problem

- unwillingness to clearly delineate who has responsibility and authority for key tasks and/or decisions across the organization

- establishing service-level agreements and then not driving accountability to achieve those agreements

- developing an organizational structure around individuals, friends, or personal biases instead of one based on the structure that is most appropriate to execute your mission

The implementation of a new organizational structure is more complex than I could possibly cover given that the purpose of this book is to stick to simple tools for the most common change situations. If you do engage in a restructuring project, each element of the MOSAIC framework would still need to be applied at every level of the implementation process. For example, once you've selected your final structure is when the hard work begins: staffing the organization with the appropriate talent to execute your strategy, aligning all the other parts of the organization to support the new structure, managing the implementation effectively to minimize the disruption the restructuring will cause, and ensuring leaders abide by the key change principles.

Again, if there's one element of MOSAIC that lends itself to external help, it is ORGANIZE. For good reason, many leaders enlist the help of an organizational effectiveness professional to assist in the planning and execution of organizational design changes. If you are contemplating organization-level restructuring for a sizable organization, get help! Extensive restructuring is not for the faint of heart and a poorly executed effort can have a significant and negative impact on your organization.

* * *

The Foundational Tools: Who Has the X? | Service-Level Agreement Template

Chapter 4

Staff to Execute the Mission

Without the right talent, nothing happens right

Once you have the right structure in place, you need to ensure that you have the right people placed in the right roles within that structure. Several years ago, I worked with a client I'll call Max. Max was a very, very nice man. Too nice, if there is such a thing. He had been the CEO of the same company for twenty-two years. He knew every employee, and they knew him. People loved him. He was everyone's favorite uncle. In a five-year period, their industry changed, and they experienced explosive growth. As a result, they needed to do a significant restructuring to reallocate resources more appropriately to key market areas. Max did a wonderful job supporting out-of-the-box thinking about how to restructure, but he did a lousy job of evaluating his talent and placing the right people into the new organization. He struggled to remove employees who lacked the skills to step into more contemporary roles. For example, although he needed much stronger technical skills in IT, he placed his longtime golfing buddy in the role because he wasn't sure his buddy could find another role given his advanced age. Even though he needed a contemporary marketing leader with strong experience in digital marketing, he selected a finance leader who didn't have a seat remaining at the table when finance finished restructuring. These poor staffing decisions (which were based on personal allegiances and his inability to make hard decisions about talent) crippled the organization.

There are volumes written about how to staff an organization. If you are interested in best practices for creating job profiles, interviewing, hiring, et cetera, there are an abundance of materials available with a quick online search. For simplicity, I want to focus on three critical areas of talent management that are important to organizational change and tend to be managed rather poorly in most organizations:

- linking your staffing strategy to the strategic needs of the organization

- having a structured talent review process

- investing time and energy in the development of your most promising talent to ensure a strong talent pipeline

Had Max invested the time to address the three talent management activities listed above, he would have significantly altered the trajectory of his organization, all for the positive. Let's look at each of these separately.

Linking Your Staffing Strategy to the Strategic Needs of the Organization

Have I mentioned that everything is dependent on your mission? When there is any change in your mission, you should pause and consider what, if anything, would require a change in your approach to staffing and talent management. For example, when the PAX-Z executive team was building their plan-on-a-page, they realized just how far behind they were on using technology to better meet their customers' needs and produce better products. Additionally, they realized that their shift in strategy had clear staffing implications. As you can see from the PAX-Z example below, by taking the time to consider the staffing implications for each for their four strategic outcomes, they were able to identify specific skill gaps that they would need to address to execute their overall mission.

Organization and People Capability Requirements: PAX-Z Three-Year Strategy

Strategic Outcomes	**Organization Capability:** *What is the current organization capability versus what will be needed to achieve the strategy (e.g., clear success metrics, well-defined accountability for results, rewards in place to drive the right behaviors, MOS, lateral integration, efficient deployment of work)?* **People Capability:** *What is the current people capability versus what will be needed to achieve the strategy (e.g., quality of talent, appropriateness of skill mix given current versus future requirements)?*				
	What Is Our Current Situation?	**Competencies Required to Achieve Our Plan**	**Develop or Acquire?**	**Actions to be Taken**	**Owner / Due Date**
Realigned and more Focused Portfolio of Products	• Our current portfolio is too broad given our size, and it is impacting our profit margins. • Current customers are demanding high-tech golf equipment, and right now, it is difficult for us to compete.	• Deeper customer knowledge	Develop	• Identify external resources with expertise in the recreational golf arena to help us better understand the market we should serve	Gert– Sept. 10
Robust Marketing & Brand Strategy	• We are predominately US based, with some reach into Canada and Japan. We are virtually unknown in Europe, Australia, or other parts of SE Asia. • We are poorly represented on the internet and/or social media.	• Deep knowledge of recreational golfers in the markets where we want to expand • Knowledge and skills in use of social media to target identified markets	Acquire Develop	• Recruit talent within targeted regions • Conduct a workshop for PAX-Z employees on best practices for using social media • Source recreational golfers to participate in a marketing survey to better understand equipment needs and wants	Maggie— Oct. 12 Maggie— Dec. 4 Gert— Sept. 30
Technology Roadmap	• We do not have the requisite competencies. • We are "old-school" in our approaches. • We are behind from an equipment and technology perspective.	• Engineering skills and competencies in AI, physics, 3D printing, and advanced manufacturing technologies	Acquire	• Identify specific universities and/or tech schools for recruiting opportunities • Establish an internship program for select AI, physics, 3D printing, and advanced manufacturing technologies undergrads	Maggie— Nov. 11 Maggie— April 1
Cost-effective Manufacturing	• We lack process discipline and operational excellence skills inside the organization. • We have outdated equipment in multiple locations that is costly to maintain.	• Operational excellence, lean manufacturing, and/or Six Sigma skills	Develop internally and acquire	• Identify people within the organization who have an interest in these areas and would be able to skill up quickly and contribute (Hugh Budd?) • Recruit a Six Sigma Black Belt with an engineering background	Fred to work with Vicki— Oct. 20

This doesn't have to be a complex process. As part of the annual strategic planning process, I suggest that clients complete the simple template on the prior page. This enables them to consider each of the strategic outcomes from their plan-on-a-page, drive a discussion of the staffing implications, and put plans in place to address any gaps. Again, keep the conversation simple. You aren't trying to overwhelm the human resources department with new staffing requirements. You are looking for the most critical staffing implications based on changes in your overall strategic plan. If nothing has really changed in your strategy, just acknowledge that and move on. Then make it an intentional and annual activity.

Having a Structured Talent Review Process

There are many firms that specialize in very robust talent management tools. They even have good online tracking systems so you can create easy-to-access databases of your talent. If you can afford them, those are a great way to access talent data. However, an overreliance on the tools can prevent you from the core goals of good talent management practices: to identify, develop, and retain talent that is critical to the future success of your organization!

Good talent management is made easier by digital tracking tools, but it doesn't require expensive tools. What it does require is the right leaders getting in a room and having open, honest, and high-quality conversations about the talent in their organization.

A good talent management process should enable you to answer questions such as:

- Which employees are most critical to our future?

- Which employees must we retain to stay competitive?

- Have the necessary steps been taken to ensure we can retain them?

- Which employees can move up in the organization to take on higher levels of responsibility?

- Do those employees have clear development plans so they are ready to step up when we need them?

- Where do we have poor performers that subtract more than they add in terms of value to the company?

- Are we taking the appropriate action to either improve their performance or replace them with a more value-added employee?

- Where do we have good employees who may be in the wrong role?

- Where do we have employees who would add more value and/or be reenergized if we placed them in a different role within the organization?

I've worked with clients who invest quite heavily in very structured talent review processes. Each year, they will spend several months of time assessing and reviewing talent. Don't get me wrong. I think any time invested by leaders in discussing their most critical asset (people) is generally time well spent, but I have also seen it get out of hand. You don't need thirty slides to have a good talent review conversation. I'd suggest that a leadership discussion around three key topics generally serves the purpose. If you want to implement a basic and structured talent review process, consider topics starting with:

1. ABC Talent Discussion

2. Succession Replacement Table

3. Retention, Moves, and Single Points of Failure

These three areas should be part of any good talent management process. Let's look at each one in more detail.

The ABC Talent Discussion

When I was young, I had a myriad of jobs: a paper route, clearing tables in a steak house, and selling root beer and burgers at an A&W, where I'd never seem to wash the smell of french fries out of my clothes. And then I worked my way through college as a bank teller. It was my first real exposure to a large group of adults in a professional working environment. There were about fifteen people in the office. Even at that tender age, it didn't take me long to spot the hard workers from the coasters.

We had Dolores, who always showed up early and always stayed late. She was the go-to person for any question you might have. If you didn't know about something, you could be sure that she did. Honestly, that office would have fallen apart without her. She was an A player, one of the best performers; she delivered above-average results, was a pleasure to work with, and everyone knew it.

Cammy was a very solid performer. She was steady and reliable and would consistently meet and sometimes exceed her expected results. When she felt valued as an employee and felt good about the organization, she'd deliver 100 percent. If she felt that the organization wasn't taking care of her, she'd be more selective about how she invested her discretionary time. She was what I'd call a B player.

And then there was Kenny. He was the last one in in the morning and first one out of the door at night. He would be late, get reprimanded, and get put on notice to improve his results over the next ninety days. And guess what? He'd improve. But only for ninety days. Then he'd fail to deliver results and revert to his old behaviors. I felt bad for my boss. She spent significant time managing him and it required a LOT of paperwork. He was clearly a C player and since the other tellers and I ended up doing most of his work,

I often wondered if we would just be better off without him. He was a complete drain on the organization and on our customers.

I share this story with you because I am a firm believer that two A players are worth more than four C players and you manage them differently. You invest in your A players. They are critical to your future talent pipeline and can take your organization to new heights when they are well managed. You replace your C players because they will pull your organization down, not lift it. To take either of those actions, you must take the time to identify and categorize your talent.

Forced Ranking

One of the most common methods of categorizing your talent is something known as "forced ranking" or a "vitality curve". It is a process of evaluating employees' work performance based on their comparison with peers instead of against fixed performance standards. Many organizations use some version of a forced ranking system to differentiate their talent and distribute compensation. It's basically a process of dividing employees into groups and placing them on a nine-box grid. As you can see with the example on the next page, the grid has *x*- and *y*-axes that indicate the dimensions you want to evaluate. You can choose whatever dimensions you want, but most grids use results and then one other dimension, such as potential, behaviors, and/or values. Placement on the grid helps you differentiate the performance of your staff. In this example, boxes two, three, and six are generally your highest performers. I'm often asked how a box-six placement can be considered a high performer. This box indicates standard results and above-average behaviors. Generally employees who are new to their roles, dealing with temporary assignments, unfamiliar with the work, and/or are high potential but haven't been in their jobs long enough to achieve above-average results can also find their way into this cell. Box six presents a leader with the opportunity to still consider above-average compensation for these individuals.

An illustration of the PAX-Z Talent Assessment is shown on the next page. This is a sample of using a forced ranking tool to place each of Sam's level two leaders in a specific block on the grid.

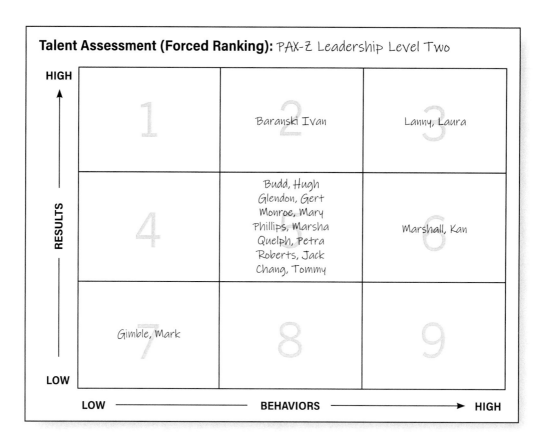

Succession planning is the process of identifying and developing future talent so that you have a ready talent pipeline when needed. Forced ranking can be a very useful tool for succession planning, and although it is commonly used in many companies, it has become controversial for several reasons.

In many companies today, forced ranking tools have shifted from an objective assessment of talent to become a vehicle for the distribution and justification of incentives. Those in high boxes are compensated better than those in lower boxes. That may work when you have accurately placed employees on the grid, but in many companies, the desire to save money has managers doing it backward. The placement is made to justify the salary rather than making the placement and then compensating appropriately.

If the use of a forced ranking tool is not well-managed, it can create a competitive culture where employees invest more time in self-promotion to gain better placement on the grid, rather than collaborating with their peers. Over the years I have seen far too many companies use forced ranking to justify cost reduction; developing a budget and then pressuring managers to ensure a certain percentage of employees are placed in each box regardless of their actual performance or behavior. I believe that when you use forced ranking in that way, you lose leadership credibility and damage the psychological contract with your employees that leadership will make every effort to treat them fairly. When employees are forced into a box to meet annual merit budgets, they know it's not a fair process. The message you are really sending is that how they perform doesn't influence how they are rewarded, which is absolutely the wrong message if you want to drive high employee engagement and improved performance.

If leaders use forced ranking tools appropriately and with integrity, they can drive the right conversations and be very helpful in differentiating your talent. They can also lead you to make appropriate decisions about how to best manage your workforce. However, I strongly believe that small companies should run as fast as they can away from forced ranking. I have seen incredibly collaborative cultures fall apart when this process is misused. Should you have a good discussion on talent? Absolutely. Do you need to use forced ranking to have that conversation? Absolutely not.

If you want to explore a forced ranking process, there are multiple tools available online. Personally, I do not advocate using forced ranking for any compensation decisions due to the high level of misuse I have seen with the tool. However, I am a strong advocate of using a simple, ABC ranking method to provide a discussion framework for leaders to identify, develop, and manage their talent. I generally encourage leadership teams to categorize their talent using the following definitions.

ABC Talent Definitions	
A	Individuals who consistently **exceed performance expectations.** They contribute to a greater degree than expected in order to achieve organizational goals. They give 120 percent effort to any assignment. When you need to involve an employee in work and you must ensure that they will deliver on an assignment, these are the people you will call. These are your go-to employees.
B	Individuals who demonstrate <u>steady, consistent performance</u> that **meets expectations.** They effectively apply technical skills and knowledge to get the job done and ensure that organizational goals are met. They give 80–100 percent effort and are the heartbeat of the organization. B is a strong placement and means the organization values such consistent contribution.
C	Individuals whose performance is **below expectations.** They give <80 percent effort, and their work requires regular guidance and monitoring. C describes substandard performance and inconsistent contribution and effort. Specific, repeated examples of unsatisfactory performance have been communicated to the staff member both verbally and in writing along with specific expectations and suggestions for improvement, but it fails to result in sustained performance improvements.

A simple approach to conducting a talent conversation is outlined below:

1. First, be very selective about whom you involve in the talent discussion. Typically it is a leader who works with their team to conduct a review of the next level down. Let's look at the PAX-Z organization chart below. Sam has six direct reports. A typical talent review conversation would involve Sam and his six direct reports. The target of the review would be to discuss everyone who reports to someone on Sam's executive team (the level-two leadership team).

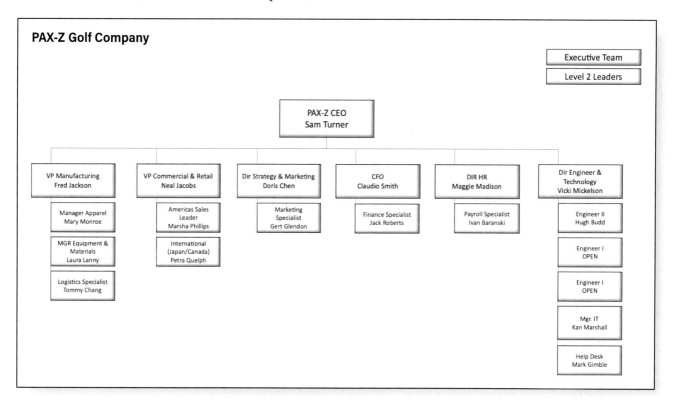

2. Make a sheet with three columns of A, B, and C.

3. Discuss the overall purpose of the exercise and the how the team should think about the ABC categorization. (Review the ABC definitions provided in the chart on page 39.)

4. Review the ground rules you'd like the team to abide by during the discussion. Some commonly used ground rules are included in the sample on the next page. Get the team to agree to the ground rules before moving forward. If anyone disagrees, engage in the appropriate level of discussion required to align on the ground rules before moving forward.

SAMPLE: Talent Discussion Ground Rules

TALENT DISCUSSION GROUND RULES

As a leadership team, we need to openly discuss our talent so that we can identify where we should invest in additional development for key talent and identify those whom we may need to move and/or shift to other roles (to improve our organization's performance). Therefore we will remember to adhere to the following ground rules throughout the conversation.

· You are not here to represent and/or protect your subordinates.

· Don't provide politically correct feedback. We want open and honest conversation, so don't hold back!

· We all change over the course of our careers, so be cautious about "old tapes" you play on any individual employee. They may have changed since you worked with them, so ask for recent feedback.

· Be open to alternative thoughts about the employee's talent and contribution. You may think they are out-standing, but others may disagree, so be equally open to less favorable reviews.

· If you offer thoughts about the employee's contribution, they should be based on direct experience, not secondhand information. Comments such as "I've heard X about Sam" aren't allowed.

> **This discussion is CONFIDENTIAL and cannot be shared with anyone outside of the room, including the employee. Do not share your input or the input of anyone else in the room!**

---

5. Before you have any group discussion, ask each leader to quietly place their suggested employee ratings into the appropriate ABC column. (If you are together in a room, put each employee name on an individual sticky note so that it can be moved based on the discussion. If the meeting is virtual, collect the input prior to the meeting and then show the chart.) Before you begin the discussion, you should have a chart (with everyone's initial input) like the PAX-Z example shown on the following page.

ABC Talent Discussion: Level-Two Leadership Team

A—Consistently Exceeds Expectations (Critical Talent, Must Keep)	B—Meets Expectations (Steady and Consistent Performer)	C—Below Expectations (Limited Impact if Exited)
Ivan Baranski Laura Lanny	Hugh Budd Gert Glendon Kan Marshall Mary Monroe Marsha Phillips Petra Quelph Jack Roberts Tommy Chang	Mark Gimble

6. After all the stickies are placed, conduct a "by-exception" review. Give everyone time to review the initial placements and then ask if there are any names that the team feels are placed in the wrong column.

7. Facilitate an open discussion on employees as presented by their leaders, focusing on any areas of disagreement.

8. Continue to ensure that the team is clear on the definitions for each column as outlined on page 39.

9. Work with the team to arrive at a final ABC list.

10. Remind everyone of the importance of keeping the conversation confidential.

When conducting talent reviews, don't rush through it. It is important to leave the conversation with everyone feeling that they had sufficient time to represent their perspectives and hear others' perspectives. Here are some things to keep in mind as you work to finalize the list:

• Leaders will feel protective of their teams, but don't allow the leaders to move everyone into the A category. The As generally represent the top 10–15 percent of the employee population. (So if you have twenty people in your organization, you'll generally only have one or two in the A column.)

• If you want to develop a strong talent pipeline, it is important to differentiate between the As and Bs. Bs will represent the majority of your employees, but your A talent will require an investment so be selective about who is categorized as an A!

REMEMBER: The intention of the ABC talent assessment exercise is not to argue for hours about who has the right to be in a certain box. It also isn't about defending your talent. The best talent conversations are open and honest acknowledgements of how your staff is performing. A good talent review surfaces hidden talent and allows you to clearly define the most critical talent for additional investment so that you can prepare them for future responsibilities.

Talent reviews are best when facilitated by an objective third party, so having your human resource manager or another skilled and objective facilitator lead these discussions is always better than doing it on your own. This will help leaders avoid looking like they are slanting the conversation more positively toward any one employee being discussed.

Succession Replacement Tables

It continues to surprise me how frequently clients experience the loss of an employee and yet have given very little thought to a possible replacement. A succession replacement table is used to help leaders think about current roles, evaluate the depth and availability of the talent pipeline to fill those roles if the need arises, and identify gaps that need to be addressed to ensure a robust succession pipeline. It isn't complex; it just takes discipline to complete it on a regular schedule so that the organization can take the right actions and avert potential staffing crises. A sample succession replacement table for the PAX-Z executive team is shown below.

Succession Replacement Table: PAX-Z Executive Team

Current Role	Incumbent	Top Candidate	Interested	"Ready Now" Candidates	Ready in One to Two Years	Ready in Three to Five Years
Director of Human Resources	Madison, Maggie	Baranski, Ivan	Y	Baranski, Ivan	Brown, James Marvel, Mary	Rally, Art
Manager of Engineering and Technology	Vicki Mickelson	Marshall, Kan	Y	Simms, Malcolm Marshall, Kan	Smith, Joe	Allen, Janet Moe, Lisa
VP of Commercial and Retail	Jacobs, Neal	Quelph, Petra	Y	Quelph, Petra	Cruise, Cassie Dancy, Tim Phillips, Marsha	Gimble, Mark Bennett, Dave
Strategy and Marketing Director	Chen, Doris	External Search	-			Glendon, Gert Phillips, Marsha
VP of Manufacturing	Jackson, Fred	External Search	-		Dancy, Tim Lanny, Laura	Budd, Hugh Pierce, Paul
CFO	Smith, Claudio	Jacobs, Neal	N	Mickelson, Vicki		Roberts, Jack

NOTE: Do not leave the "top candidate" box empty. If "ready now" candidates are listed, there must be a candidate listed as the top candidate.

Through this simple exercise, you can easily identify gaps in succession. For example, as you can see from Sam's executive team replacement table, two of the six roles on his staff have no "ready now" internal candidates. So if either Doris or Fred left the organization, the company would have to promote someone who wasn't ready or conduct an external search. But by completing this proactive assessment, the team could take either of the following actions: accelerate the development of internal talent that is identified but not listed as "ready now" or attempt to recruit external talent into another role so that they have talent in the organization before there is a direct need to replace Doris or Fred.

Succession replacement tables can be used at any level of the organization, but they are generally completed for all levels of leadership to mitigate the potential risk if a leader departs quickly. To complete a succession replacement table, follow the steps outlined below:

1. List all the jobs currently on the leadership team (or whatever level you are assessing).

2. List the current incumbent in the role.

3. Brainstorm any potential replacement candidates.

   a. Think broadly about potential candidates. For example, if you are assessing the marketing leadership team, consider any candidates with prior marketing experience regardless of whether they are currently working in the marketing organization.

   b. Think externally. Are there people you know outside the organization who might be interested in and/or qualified for the role? Consider candidates who may be currently working for your competition. Or consider people whom you know from professional organizations.

   c. Be open to nontraditional candidates, but don't include long shots on the final list. (Let's be honest: I'd like Tom Brady to play on my weekend football team, but it isn't likely to happen, so when completing a replacement table for your organization, ensure that the list is comprised of realistic candidates.)

4. Move to the right of the chart and populate the three further columns with a viable list of final candidates.

5. From the list of "ready now" candidates, identify the top candidate and place that person's name in the third column. (If you had to choose tomorrow, who would you choose? This may change in next year's review, but make a choice so if something happens, you'll be prepared.)

6. If someone in the group has firsthand knowledge that the individual would be interested in the role, put a yes or "Y" in the fourth column. If you don't know, find a way to discover what, if any, interest the person may have in the role should it become available in the future (without making any promises).

NOTE: This is an important point. I often see clients blindly make career plans for their employees without ever discussing it with them. Employees accept and/or decline jobs for a multitude of reasons. Don't assume that you know. If they are uninterested and/or unwilling to take a role you have planned for them, find out sooner rather than later so you can make alternate plans. If you have someone who is clearly the top candidate but is not interested in the role, you still need to know that. Would it help pique their interest if the CEO had a conversation about the role?

Retention, Moves, and Single Points of Failure (SPOFs)

Retention, moves, and single points of failure are three areas that can produce a rich dialogue and yield valuable insights for your talent management efforts. You can put it on multiple slides, but in general, you won't have a lot of names on this list, so I tend to keep it on a single chart. A sample assessment for the PAX-Z Leadership Level Two is shown below.

Retention, Moves, and Single Points of Failure: PAX-Z Leadership Levels One and Two

Retention—Do we have anyone this team who is likely to leave in the next six months?

Name	Current Role	Individual Risk (H/M/L)	Organization Risk (H/M/L)	Issue	Recommended Actions
Gert Glendon	Marketing Specialist	H	M	Gert is highly marketable and has received several other lucrative offers in the last six months for new marketing roles.	Evaluate his current compensation and place him on a possible long-term retention plan if appropriate.

Moves—Who might benefit from an internal job move?

Name and Role	Rationale and Recommended Action
Jack Roberts (Finance Specialist)	He has been in the role for sixteen years and needs to be more challenged. Give him process management training so he can expand his skill set and we can improve financial process discipline.

Single Points of Failure—Do we have any single points of failure?

Name and Role	Recommended Action
Mark Gimble (Help Desk)	Launch an immediate search for an external hire to ensure a "ready now" backfill.
Laura Lanny (Manager of Equipment and Materials)	Put a development plan in place for Laura to accelerate her development for her next role. Hire a strategic backfill.

Retention

The intent of this chart is to create a dialogue on three key talent challenges: where you may have potential retention risks, who might benefit from moving to another role inside the organization, and where you have any single points of failure (SPOFs) that need immediate attention.

A typical approach to completing the retention, moves, and single points of failure chart is outlined below.

1. List the name of any employee who you think is a real retention risk. List their current role.

2. Provide an honest assessment of how likely it is that the person will leave. Is the risk high, medium, or low? If their spouse is taking a new job and is moving to another state next month, I'd call that a certain and therefore high risk. If they seem somewhat dissatisfied in their job but you have no direct information that they will leave, it may be temporary and therefore a low risk.

3. Next, provide an assessment of the level of impact to the organization if the person left. Is the risk high, medium, or low? Could you easily replace the person? If so, the risk is probably low. If you have no one else in the organization who would be able to step in and do the job, that is likely to be a high risk to the organization.

    NOTE: Be careful here. I've seen leaders try to leverage this exercise to get the individual more money by exaggerating the real retention risk. That is bad for both the organization and the individual. It is one thing to surface a possible retention risk, but don't misuse this. If the leadership team is constantly worried that an individual may leave, they will find other options to replace that person, and you will have done them a disservice by misrepresenting the real level of risk. Also, keep in mind that all employees aren't worthy of extensive retention efforts. If an employee continually sends messages that they don't want to stay, let them go. Sometimes it is more important to focus on a good succession plan than it is to continually try to retain individuals who are chronically at high risk of leaving.

4. Briefly document why the individual is a retention risk. What are the contributing factors? Is it a compensation issue? A job-satisfaction issue? Would they be leaving for personal reasons, such as a spouse job move or an eldercare issue?

5. Finally, include any recommended actions to be taken. If you don't want to retain the person, suggest that no actions be taken. If you do want to retain the individual, suggest options such as those listed below.

    a. If it is compensation related, can you make salary or incentive adjustments?

b. If it is a job satisfaction issue, can you modify or expand the role in any way? Can you provide an additional job assignment to further develop the individual's skills?

c. If their spouse is moving, could you offer a remote working arrangement?

Moves

Sometimes a good employee just needs a change of scenery. A temporary and/or permanent job change can do wonders to reenergize a longtime employee while allowing critical knowledge to remain in the organization albeit in a new role. This is an opportunity for the leadership team to discuss who might benefit from an internal move and/or job expansion.

1. List any individuals who might benefit from an internal move and/or job expansion.

2. Define the reason for suggesting a move and any specific suggestions on potential moves that might be a fit. Think it through and be specific. As you can see from the PAX-Z example on page 45, Jack Roberts is a good employee who has been in his role for sixteen years. That's a long time. He is a solid B player but might even be an A player if he could get reenergized with a new challenge. Claudio has suggested expanding his role to include process mapping. This is a good example of role expansion for a good employee.

Single Points of Failure (SPOFs)

An SPOF is a term often used by technical organizations to describe a part of a system that, if it fails, will stop the entire system from working and/or is likely to provoke a total systems failure in case of malfunction. SPOFs are undesirable in any system that wants to achieve high reliability. This concept is equally applicable to staffing. Do you have people in your organization who are critical to the organization, and if they chose to leave, you would have no way to complete the work they do?

For example, let's go back to the PAX-Z example on page 45. Laura Lanny currently runs the equipment and materials organization. She is an A player who has been in the role for twelve years, has a big, complicated job, and no one else in the organization knows how to do it. It would be a huge loss for PAX-Z if Laura chose to leave. Mark Gimble runs the IT help desk. He is a C player, but he is also the only one who knows how to respond to the IT issues other employees need resolved. They are very different types of employees, but both Laura Lanny and Mark Gimble are identified as SPOFs because no one else in the organization can currently step in to do their roles. Therefore, it is important to develop an action plan for both.

1. On the bottom right section of the chart, identify any SPOFs in your part of the organization.

2. Finally list any recommended actions to address the issue. Again, be specific. Listing something like "Resolve the issue with Mark Gimble" isn't a strong action. "Launch an immediate search for an external hire to ensure a 'ready now' backfill" is a real action that the team can agree to and immediately assign to someone.

Don't overcomplicate your talent review process! You'll find that once you get started, people want to add all kinds of other topics into the conversation. "How much diversity do we have in the organization?" "What does the internship program need to look like?" "What are you doing to support our latest initiative?" I'm not suggesting that these topics don't need to be reviewed at some point, but if you are new to talent management, get the basics down first, and then once you have a regular cadence of talent review meetings, you can begin to add additional topics.

Develop Your Most Promising Talent to Ensure a Strong Talent Pipeline

I wish I had a dime for every leader that told me, "My people are my most important asset." I always want to believe that is true. One CEO told me how much he cared about his talent and how much he had invested in his employees in the three years he had been running the company. They even had a talent management program that promised that the CEO would spend one hour a year with each of the most promising A players in the organization. The goal was to have the CEO invest time to talk with them about their career and future with the company. It sounded great!

A month into the engagement, I found out that the CEO had refused to spend the promised one hour a year with those high-performing employees. His view was, "I already talk to them a lot, and I'm busy." I was shocked.

It has been my experience that leaders frequently proclaim that they value their people, but their actions would indicate quite the opposite. They will buy a $50,000 piece of equipment and invest time and money to maintain that equipment. They will oil it. They will polish it. They will do an annual maintenance check-up to ensure it is running smoothly. Yet they will have hundreds of employees with salaries far beyond that $50,000 investment and yet struggle to find an hour during the year to have an open conversation with the employee about their needs, concerns, or career aspirations. I don't get it. Organizations are comprised of people, and nothing happens in your organization without people. Leaders should never forget that talent truly is your most important investment.

Employees are just like that piece of equipment. If you don't maintain the relationship, and if you don't invest in them, they will begin to wonder if they are valued. Don't get me wrong. I am not suggesting a lot of "touchy-feely" time with employees or increasing everyone's compensation. Far from it. I am suggesting that you invest time with your talent. This is especially true for your A players. If you want to retain them, you need to maintain the relationship in such a way that they want to stay in your organization.

Your A players are your best bets to ensure the next generation of both technical and managerial leadership. Invest time in them. Talk to them. Understand what they aspire to do in their career. Prepare them to take on bigger roles with more responsibility. Unfortunately, if you don't, the good ones will find options outside your organization. The bad ones will stay because they have no options.

Several years ago I had a client who wanted to put a program in place to develop her leaders. Let's call her Sally. I asked for a list of the talent that she wanted to develop, and she produced her complete organization chart. Twenty-one people were on her list. I asked her if every one of those employees was worth developing. I think she was surprised. She felt that it was her duty as a leader to develop everyone on the team. And she was worried that it would look like playing favorites if she didn't invest in developing everyone. If Sally had had unlimited resources, her plan would have been great. But I have yet to meet a leader with an unlimited budget. In my experience, C players will always be C players. Investing in them is generally not productive. Sally needed to identify two specific target groups for her development efforts.

First, her most critical future talent. The A players that, if managed well, would continue to move through the organization, taking on more and more responsibility and building the skills necessary to lead at higher levels. Second, she needed to identify the replacement candidates for those SPOFs. For both groups (A players and SPOF replacement candidates), you should establish more formalized development plans. An individual development plan (IDP) doesn't have to be a time-consuming task. You can work with the employee to build it, ask the employee to implement it as planned, and then establish a quarterly review meeting to check in on their progress.

There is an endless string of research studies on why people are attracted to and/or stay with an organization. Although you'll see some slight variation across the studies, the general finding is that people stay with organizations for two primary reasons: (1) they like their direct boss, and (2) they feel valued and have an opportunity to develop their skills. In most of the studies, compensation is generally the third factor. This is a significant finding because it indicates that a good relationship with the boss and opportunities to learn will do more to retain employees than throwing money at them. If you want to send a message that you value an employee, an individual development plan is a great place to start. I would suggest that individual development plans get built for all your A players and any SPOF replacement candidates. A sample individual development plan is included on the following page.

Building a Robust Development Plan

Let's look at what constitutes a good development plan. Shown below is the development plan for Laura Lanny, our PAX-Z project manager.

Individual Development Plan

Name: Laura Lanny		**Job Title:** Manager of Equipment and Materials	
Date: January 15, 20xx		**Mentor (if applicable):** Neal Jacobs	
Development Area	**Development Action(s)**	**How will it be measured?**	**Due Date**
Demonstrate Strategic Leadership	• Colead manufacturing consolidation project with Fred Jackson • Meet with the Americas sales leader (Marsha Phillips) to learn the basics of pricing strategy	• Feedback from initiative partner • Meeting complete	End of year June 22
Improve Financial Acumen	• Attend each quarterly analyst meeting and then meet with the CFO to discuss learnings • Attend finance for the nonfinancial executive program offered through OSU	• Quarterly meetings complete • Class complete	June 30 April 1
Gain Presentation and Media-Relations Skills	• Set up a session with media expert to strengthen media/formal presentation skills • Observe others who excel in this area to identify any applicable tips or techniques (Doris Chen)	• Session complete • Observations complete and applied and feedback discussed with Doris	March 18 July 23

Often leaders will send employees to a training class for development or suggest the employee read a book. There is nothing wrong with that, but if you've been around awhile, you know that most real learning doesn't happen in a classroom or from reading a book. Think back to the key learning experiences you have had over the course of your career. I would bet they didn't happen in a classroom. Learning comes in all forms, and yes, you can absolutely learn in a classroom, but don't discount other learning experiences, such as:

- taking on a temporary stretch assignment beyond your day-to-day work;

- being part of a team that is working on a project that has nothing to do with your current role (e.g., an HR employee spending the day in a call center to better understand the customer experience);

- meeting once a month with a mentor who specializes in an area where you need development (e.g., building financial skills through a mentoring relationship with a skilled finance leader);

- taking on a leadership role in an industry or professional association (e.g., volunteering to help set up a large conference for your professional organization to improve your event-planning skills);

- attending a webinar or reading a relevant book and presenting your learnings to a peer team (what critical issues is your business facing? who are the experts that you can learn from and then share those learnings back with the organization?); or

- serving on a due-diligence acquisition team.

Each of the items above is an example of the variety of experiences you can put on a development plan. Be creative and think out-of-the-box. Ask the employee what they think would be helpful. And it is important not to overload the plan. Select no more than two to three development areas, build appropriate development experiences, and then follow up. As you can see from Laura Lanny's plan, of the six development actions, only two are scheduled to happen in a classroom. All the others are more experiential and on-the-job development.

One part of development planning that should be considered is the option of assigning a mentor to the individual being developed. An ideal mentor is a leader who will:

- have a genuine desire to assist in the development of others;

- bring role-model leadership behaviors into the mentoring relationship, allowing the mentee to observe what "good" looks like;

- dedicate time and energy to the mentoring relationship (at least quarterly) to provide coaching and advice;

- invest time in understanding and removing obstacles to the mentee's personal and professional development;

- protect the confidentiality of the mentor/mentee discussions;

- serve as a sounding board for how the mentee should approach sticky situations; and

- commit to a minimum of a one-year mentoring relationship to ensure consistency in the development process.

The right type of mentor can be a lifeline to your top talent. When your A players are approached about external roles, the mentoring relationship can tether them more strongly to your organization. But don't assign mentors blindly. Talk to the employee about their interest in a potential mentoring relationship. Ask them for three potential mentors, then select the most appropriate person based on the specific development needs of the employee and the mentor criteria list above. And ensure that the mentor understands and is ready to fulfill the role of the mentor, actively engaging with the employee to support their development.

Summary

So based on this chapter, here are the common pitfalls to avoid in the "S" or STAFF component of the MOSAIC framework:

- failing to link your staffing strategy to the strategic needs of the organization

- not having a robust talent review process that enables you to identify your top talent

- failing to invest time and energy in the development of your most promising talent to ensure a talent pipeline for the future

Do you already have a robust talent management review process? If so, great! If not, get started by focusing on the three areas identified above. Invest the time necessary to understand the talent implications of your strategy, implement a simple three-topic talent review process, put plans in place to develop your A players and build plans to address your SPOFs.

Investing just a small amount of time in talent management will serve as a force multiplier for your organization. When done well, it increases leadership credibility, it improves employee retention, and it establishes a robust talent pipeline.

Perhaps the most significant factor in establishing a talent development process is the commitment from the leadership team (not just human resources) to execute to the talent management plan. If the leadership team isn't fully committed to investing the right level of time in talent management, then don't do it. A partial effort will signal to the organization a lack of commitment to employee development. And it will set expectations within the organization that the leadership team is unable to meet, so don't initiate any type of development program unless you intend to follow through.

* * *

The Foundational Tools: Organization & People Capability Requirements | ABC Talent Discussion | Succession Replacement Table | Retention, Moves, and Single Points of Failure | Individual Development Plan

> Important: Talent management practices, including how you engage in conversations about employees and how you use and store these forms, need to comply with all applicable labor laws for your country, state, or region of the world. Please check with your legal counsel prior to the use of these tools to ensure you are compliant with the laws in your area.

Chapter 5

Align the Organization

If you don't use the right glue, your change won't stick!

I received a request once from a CEO who wanted to pay me six figures to design and implement "team training" for the top two layers of his organization. Let's call him Henry. Henry had just returned from a Harvard leadership seminar where team training (which was a big trend at the time) was presented as the solution to a high level of internal infighting. He had observed that his employees were not very collaborative across the boundaries of the organization, and he thought that putting them all through training on how to be a better team would solve the problem. So I asked him one simple question: "Is your merit based on individual or team performance?"

Let's look at why this question is important. Henry's answer was that "each employee received an annual review of their individual performance and was compensated individually." If I had spent three months training all his employees on "teaming," Henry would have been out of a lot of money, and nothing would have changed in his organization. Why? Because the issue he was facing had nothing to do with training or a lack of employee skill. His desire to have employees shift from competitive to collaborative behavior needed to be continually reinforced by a reward system that punished competitive behaviors and reinforced collaborative behaviors. With an individually based reward system, his employees were focused primarily on what they accomplished individually, not collectively. However, if his employees were rewarded based on what the team accomplished, they would be more inclined to perform as a team. Basically his reward system was out of alignment with the change he was trying to drive. That alignment was part of the "glue" that would help Henry sustain the collaborative behaviors he wanted to see in his organization.

In a piece of mosaic art, all the tiles are held together by mortar or grout. That mortar serves as the glue that holds all the individual pieces together over time. This simple idea also applies to change within your organization. If you want the change to last, you need to assess the foundational elements of the organization and ask yourself, "Is this part of the organization set up to reinforce or to work against the change I am trying to make?"

Any element that is not currently supporting the change needs to be modified to do so. This alignment component of the MOSAIC framework is about building the "glue" that creates the "stickiness" that is ultimately required to sustain your change efforts over time. This includes aligning key stakeholders, understanding the impact of the change on customers and other parts of the organization, making modifications to employees' goals, developing new ways of rewarding employees, changing current policies and practices, and establishing and/or revising current processes. Let's explore each of these in more detail using examples from the PAX-Z Golf Company.

Today PAX-Z has five manufacturing facilities for the company: four in the United States and one in Canada. They have a sales office in Japan but no manufacturing outside of North America. Over time each of the five site managers has developed a variety of processes specific to their site. There is limited standardization and excessive cost because equipment must be duplicated at every site. PAX-Z is growing quickly, acquiring a new company every eighteen months, and each acquired company also has its own manufacturing processes. As a result, production at PAX-Z is complex, requires more staff than it should, and makes it challenging to fully integrate newly acquired companies. Sam, the PAX-Z CEO, quickly realized that if the company wanted to continue to grow, it would be important to centralize manufacturing into one location and then revisit that decision if the company grew outside of North America. He asked Fred Jackson, VP of manufacturing, and Laura Lanny (who works for Fred) to move forward on centralizing manufacturing for PAX-Z. This would be a significant change for the organization. Each of the tools on the following pages illustrates how Fred and Lanny worked to ensure alignment across the organization for the change they were now responsible for executing.

Stakeholder Management

A stakeholder is an individual and/or group who has an interest in and/or is affected by the change project and its outcomes. Your most critical stakeholders are people who:

- are positively and/or negatively affected by your project;

- can influence the success or failure of the change;

- can disrupt your change plans; and

- can influence others to behave and operate in ways that support or work against the change.

In 1991 Aubrey L. Mendelow, a professor from the Graduate School of Management at Kent State University, developed what came to be known as Mendelow's matrix. To this day it remains a useful tool for the analysis of stakeholders and their attitudes. Over time many people have adapted Mendelow's model, but the central premise of his work continues to be valuable when planning for organizational change. It takes a lot of time to manage people's expectations about a change, so it is important to distinguish between all stakeholders and those that you must actively manage. The bottom line is that some stakeholders matter more than others.

As you can see from the illustration below, Mendelow's matrix allows you to categorize your stakeholders into four key categories and then manage each category differently.

Stakeholder Assessment: Mendelow's Matrix (Adapted)

H	**CONSULT THEM** **Goal:** Keep them satisfied with your progress	**ENGAGE THEM** **Goal:** Get their buy-in and involve them prior to making final decisions
	MONITOR THEM **Goal:** Invest time only if it matters to your key stakeholders	**INFORM THEM** **Goal:** Show consideration and provide after-the-fact updates
L	**L** ← Level of Interest in the Change → **H**	

Influence/Power to Disrupt Change (vertical axis, L to H)

A stakeholder assessment is a tool that allows you to both categorize and plan for your various stakeholders. As you can see from the PAX-Z example on the following page, Fred and Laura have identified three specific stakeholder groups: the internal PAX-Z steering committee, site production leaders, and vendors and suppliers. Based on their analysis, the first two groups will need to be actively managed. They have also done a nice job of identifying specific actions (with clear owners and due dates) to be taken to manage their identified stakeholders.

Stakeholder Assessment: Centralized Manufacturing Project

Stakeholders	Classification	What is changing for them?	What do they need to know or do?	Actions to be taken	Owner	Due date
Steering Committee (Sam, Neal, Claudio)	Consult	• The move to centralized manufacturing will impact customers and financials.	• Understand and guide the changes • Help us to assess risk and customer impact	• Set up weekly thirty-minute update calls • Set a standard agenda to drive the right level of discussion	Laura Lanny	March 23
Site Production Leaders and Their Teams	Engage	• Manufacturing is being centralized, select plants will be closed, and employees will be impacted/downsized.	• Understand the timeline for plant closures • Support the production line move (if applicable) • Plan and be prepared to receive production from closure sites	• Share the timeline and project plan for site closures • Provide regular communication on project status • Offer incentives to production leaders to ensure a smooth transition • Determine types of severance packages to offer displaced employees	Fred Jackson Maggie Madison	April 12
Vendors and Suppliers	Inform	• PAX-Z Golf is centralizing its manufacturing operations.	• Understand the timeline for plant closures	• Hold a meeting with vendors and suppliers to inform them of timeline for pending plant closures • Provide periodic updates if timeline shifts	Tommy Chang	April 12

Getting your stakeholders to understand what you need them to know and/or do differently is the first part of the "glue" you need to align the organization behind your change. I want to be clear that stakeholder management does not mean that you alter the objectives of the change to keep stakeholders happy. That is a recipe for status quo. Unhappiness generally accompanies significant change, so it is important to accept that and push forward. A stakeholder assessment is designed to help you assess who needs to be involved and/or actively engaged in your change and develop a plan to keep them aligned to the change as you implement the new way of doing things.

Work-Impact Analysis: Understanding the Impact of the Change on Customers and Daily Work

Work-impact analysis is critical "glue" for two reasons. First, understanding how daily work needs to change will help align your organizational capacity with what is required to achieve your business results. Does your change require employees to start doing new work? Stop doing current work? Transfer work to other parts of the organization or to other team members? Every organization has limited resources. You want to make sure that all of your resources are focused on the most critical work. Work planning needs to happen at the organizational level and the individual employee level.

Most organizations are not good at rebalancing the workload after a change is initiated. Leaders just launch a new change (and all the work that goes with it) and then expect the employees to absorb the new work in addition to what is currently on their plates. That is never a recipe for success. It leads to a workforce that is overwhelmed and resentful of the "do more with less" mentality that is so prevalent these days. As part of any major change, setting up a short meeting to discuss how work will be impacted by the change will help you to avoid merely adding work to the pile. It is also critical to fully understand the potential impact on customers of any work changes so that you can limit the negative impact and proactively manage your customer communications.

PAX-Z had a much longer list of items, but the example on the next page is a partial look at the organization-level work-impact analysis they completed as part of the centralized manufacturing change project. Through this process they identified work that needed to be transferred (e.g., procurement of raw materials, which was happening at multiple sites but now needed to be done in one location). They also identified work that wasn't being done but would be required to establish the Canadian Engineering Research Center, and work that should be stopped due to the impact on one of their product lines that would no longer be in production. Again, they did a nice job of having clear actions, one clear owner for the action, and a due date.

Work-Impact Analysis: Centralized Manufacturing

What Work Needs to Change?	Does the Work Need to Start, Stop, or Transfer?	What Actions Need to Be Taken	Owner	Due Date
Reduction in procurement of raw material, equipment, and related supplies from multiple sites to one central manufacturing site	Transfer	Communicate to suppliers the process changes and inform them of the new contact point within the company.	Tommy Chang	June 21
		Finance will ensure supplier invoicing and payment processes are aligned with central manufacturing.	Claudio Smith	July 16
Ramp up the Canadian Engineering Research Center	Start	Identify the additional resources to support the added workload to support the Canadian Engineering Research Center.	Maggie Madison	Aug. 18
		Evaluate the standard reports we provide to current clients across the globe. Determine what can be reused to reduce rework.	Tim Dancy	July 1
Production of PAX Pro clubs and apparel lines	Stop	Communicate to fabric suppliers the changes and inform them of the timeline.	Mary Monroe	Dec. 1
	Start	Determine disposition of current/remaining PAX Pro equipment and apparel stock.	Mary Monroe	Dec. 1

Making Modifications to Employees' Goals

Think back to every new job you've ever had. After you located the restroom, figured out where you could get lunch, and determined where you were going to have to sit all day, your next question to your new boss was likely to be, "So what do you need me to do?"

As an employee, understanding what is expected of you initiates a snowball of thoughts and effort. You say to yourself, "If that is what I need to accomplish, then how do I prioritize my work? What do I focus on first? What work can I set aside if I am short on time?" The answers to these questions will migrate into a set of goals that you are then held accountable to achieve. The pursuit of those goals will then drive your day-to-day effort. This is considered individual goal planning.

The work-impact analysis reviewed above will define the work that needs to transfer, start, or stop because of the change you are launching. The result of that analysis needs to be translated deeper into the organization and needs to clearly define what individual employees will be expected to deliver in support of the change. How will their daily work change? What will they as an individual need to transfer, start, or stop doing to sustain the change?

Many leaders think that just saying something in a town hall meeting about the importance of a change will somehow make the change come to fruition. That is like a football coach telling the players it is important to win but never discussing how each player needs to perform on the field to contribute in their own way to ensure the win. Your change plan is unlikely to be executed unless the higher-level actions are effectively translated into specific goals and objectives for each employee. That is how you secure the win.

There is so much variety in how organizations approach goal planning and performance management that it would be of little value for me to suggest any one-size-fits-all tool here. So just remember that whatever tools you use for goal planning in your organization, your change requirements need to be reflected in the goals that you set for your employees. It can be as simple as a thirty-minute discussion between a supervisor and their employee(s). It's that simple. Don't assume that employees know the priorities. Define them. Discuss them. If employees understand new requirements to support your change, that is the first step toward ensuring they actually get it done.

Rewards That Drive Alignment to Your Change

A friend once told me that "adults are children in big bodies." I initially laughed at that description, but over the years, it has proven true more times than I can count. Children (and adults) tend to operate according to their reward system. A reward system is basically a stimulus provided to alter behavior. Rewards typically serve as reinforcers to encourage desired behaviors. When you launch a change, it is important to invest time in identifying how you currently reward employees in your organization. What behaviors get acknowledged either directly (e.g., public acknowledgement in an all-employee meeting) or less indirectly (e.g., special privileges)?

Rewards are essential "glue" for any change. There are two types of rewards: extrinsic and intrinsic. In organizations, typical extrinsic rewards are given as a result of your contribution—a merit raise, a job promotion, a special bonus, an equity share in the company, et cetera. Intrinsic rewards such as praise, encouragement, work satisfaction, et cetera have no material value but can keep an employee feeling recognized and motivated. For example, when we discussed the value of having Jack Roberts, the finance specialist for PAX-Z, take on additional responsibility by stepping outside of his finance role and learn process mapping, it was a good example of an intrinsic reward. By asking Jack to expand his role into a new area, Jack is likely to feel that he is both helping the company and displaying that he is capable of taking on new responsibility. Although it is based on something that Jack internally feels, the action is the trigger for the reward.

Rewards must be set up to align with the change you are trying to implement. Here are some examples:

- If you want to drive growth, you can consider providing special bonuses (extrinsic reward) for employees who exceed growth targets. Or give verbal recognition (intrinsic reward) to the person who brought in the biggest growth numbers in a public, all-employee meeting. It will be very clear that growth behavior is going to get rewarded.

- If you want to encourage collaboration across the boundaries of the organization, don't just talk about it. Set up an incentive system (extrinsic reward) that ensures that a percentage of each leader's annual bonus is dependent on all members of the team reaching collective/shared goals. It will only take one compensation cycle for people to realize that if they operate independently and fail to collaborate, it will impact their annual bonus.

- If you want to reinforce customer-centric behavior, establish a quarterly process of public acknowledgement (intrinsic reward) for employees who demonstrate the most customer-centric work.

As illustrated, PAX-Z developed a plan to reward employees (both extrinsically and intrinsically) for moving to the new centralized manufacturing model. The team did a nice job of recommending both temporary and permanent changes to the reward system. The temporary rewards would encourage the right behaviors through the transition period, and the permanent changes would serve as "glue" that sustained the change.

Rewards Assessment: Centralized Manufacturing Project

What operational and/or behavioral changes need to be rewarded?	What temporary rewards can we offer to encourage commitment to the change?	What needs to permanently change in our reward system (i.e., approach to compensation)?	Actions to ensure alignment	Owner	Due Date
Successful Centralization of Manufacturing Footprint	Monthly "Hole-in-One—You Made it Happen" Award from Sam in the monthly town hall	Discontinue once project is complete	• Identify the award/statue and the "Hole in One Award" process for Sam to use during the town hall	Maggie with Doris	May 21
	Give all employees a set of production golf clubs and bag with company logo upon successful completion of the centralized manufacturing consolidation project	Discontinue once project is complete	• Include the gift giveaway in our weekly employee newsletter • Communicate timeline on consolidation and provide regular updates on progress	Maggie Fred J. / Laura Lanny	TBD
	Temporary milestone bonuses during transition	Our current site bonus needs to change	• Develop temporary milestone bonus program and revise the existing site performance bonus process to a shared bonus program	Maggie	June 10
Ongoing Reduction in Overall Manufacturing Costs	Offer a $500 Lightbulb Award for any cost-reduction idea that yields more than $10,000 in annual savings	Offer a $100 Lightbulb Award for any cost-reduction idea that yields more than $5,000 in annual savings	• Revise our current Lightbulb Award process to include cost-savings ideas	Maggie	June 22

Policies and Practices That Align with Your Change

I once had a client who was desperate to increase growth in his organization. He had some outstanding business leaders who worked overtime to achieve his very aggressive growth goals. After two quarters of frustrating results, he pulled the business leaders into a conference room and berated them for what he perceived to be a lack of effort to drive growth. One of the more courageous business leaders had finally had enough. He pointed out that the CEO had launched a new travel and phone-usage policy at the beginning of the year. This policy dictated that leaders could not travel more than once a month and could not exceed $125 a month in phone charges. As a result of this policy, once a business leader reached the maximum spending for the month, they stopped visiting potential clients. In isolation the phone and the travel policy was fine, but when it failed to complement the growth objective, it no longer served its purpose. This is a great example of a policy that conflicted with the change the CEO was trying to drive.

In most organizations, policies get established, put on a shelf, and forgotten. Policies are supposed to outline standard operating procedure. Generally that is a good thing. Unfortunately, too often policies and common practices become obstacles to what you are trying to change in the organization. Once you decide to implement a change, take the time to identify the gaps in your current policies and practices, and then address them before you implement the change.

As a result of the policy and practice assessment that the PAX-Z team completed, they surfaced several clear disconnects between current policies and practices and what would be required to support the overall PAX-Z plan-on-a-page, as well as the shift to centralized manufacturing. One of the best examples is the reference to their antiquated tuition assistance program. Prior to the change, employees could only receive 50 percent reimbursement for less than a dozen courses from only a few preapproved colleges. The program was out of date, and only a handful of employees took advantage of it.

After completing the PAX-Z plan-on-a-page, it become clear that the company was falling behind their competitors in technology. To successfully execute their mission and to establish a state-of-the-art, centralized manufacturing facility, they needed to accelerate their technical capabilities. Modifying their tuition reimbursement policy would accelerate employee development in the areas of artificial intelligence, physics, 3D printing, and manufacturing technology. This is a good example of a policy that was not aligned to support the change the company was trying to implement. A sample policy and practice assessment for PAX-Z is shown on the following page.

Policy and Practice Assessment: Centralized Manufacturing

What Policy or Practice May Need to Be Modified to Better Support the Change?	What is the recommended change? (Be specific)	What actions need to be taken?	Owner	Due Date
Our current training reimbursement policy is too narrow and won't allow us to develop better internal competencies required to support and embrace the needed technology changes.	• For one year, fully fund training/certifications for all employees in engineering, manufacturing, and marketing on any course related to AI, physics, 3D printing, and/or manufacturing technology. • On an ongoing basis, provide 80 percent (instead of the current 50 percent) ongoing tuition assistance for all employees pursuing a degree in AI, physics, 3D printing, and advanced manufacturing technology courses.	• Revise the tuition reimbursement policy and communicate it to employees. • Ensure that budget dollars are allocated starting with next year's budget. • Develop an approved list of schools, workshops, and/or preferred technology programs/courses and publish it for employees.	Maggie Claudio Maggie with Ivan	May 7 Oct. 14 June 18
We currently have an eight-hour shift schedule in our manufacturing facilities.	• In order to meet our customer demands (once we have a centralized manufacturing), we need to move to a two-shift schedule. • Consider initiating a four-day, ten-hour work option.	• Explore the new shift requirements and the impact on our workforce, and make final recommendations on our shift schedule in the new facility.	Laura with Maggie	July 22
We currently donate our discontinued inventory to local golf schools.	• Give all discontinued inventory (e.g., PAX Pro 105 equipment and apparel) to vendors who help us ensure a smooth transition to a centralized manufacturing model. • After we complete the project, establish a practice of giving it to employees who achieve key training milestones for technology courses.	• Establish the criteria/milestones and implement the process. • Establish the process for identification of candidates and distribution of products.	Laura Maggie	June 1 Aug. 30
We have antiquated (nonexistent) employee communication platforms and rely on word of mouth.	• Improve our ability to ensure timely communications so that we can maintain employee morale, interest, and engagement as we move to a centralized manufacturing model.	• Upgrade employee communication tools software. • Roll out new employee communication tool.	Maggie/Kan	May 14

Processes That Support the New Way of Working

I once worked on a very large two-year transformation project. When the new CEO came in, he wanted the company to shift from a global but very fragmented organization to a more centralized organization with stronger functional capabilities and standard global processes within each functional area. He knew the shift was essential to position the organization to scale. When he arrived, each leader managed their business as a self-contained unit with different ways of doing everything. And to complicate matters, the company had made two to three acquisitions a year for the past nine years and had never integrated any of them. One employee described it as operating in "the Wild, Wild West." Here is an overview:

- This organization had inadequate and inexperienced functional support. Each business unit had one functional leader for human resources, finance, IT, marketing, et cetera. These leaders were isolated within the business, were not aligned with other functional experts that they could learn from, and completely lacked upward career opportunities within their area of functional expertise.

- Business leaders aggressively competed with one another for client business because they didn't have a shared end-to-end sales process that allowed them to maximize the opportunity to sell complete, integrated solutions across the business.

- The organization had multiple processes for introducing new products to the market. Each business launched any product it wanted to introduce whenever it wanted to introduce it. Some succeeded in the marketplace, but most didn't.

- There were almost no standardized processes. For example, instead of one process for sending out client invoices, the organization had thirty-four unique processes. When the CFO wanted to automate the invoicing process to reduce the cycle time from twenty-one days to five, it was an enormous undertaking due to the variation in the customized invoicing processes across the globe.

Basically, the "Wild, Wild West" comment didn't adequately represent the extent of the challenge the CEO faced in driving the changes he wanted.

Process clarity and discipline is a critical component of establishing the "glue" that supports the new way of doing things. If you are familiar with process mapping, skip to the next section. If not, let me cover the basics.

Process mapping is also known as flowcharting. Frank Gilbreth invented the original system in the early 1900s, and it has been a widely used technique ever since. Process mapping is a planning and management tool that visually describes the flow of work. It is often used to try to decrease the time it takes to deliver a product or service by allowing you to visually examine a process for opportunities to reduce handoffs and eliminate unnecessary steps.

Over time, day-to-day processes can become part of the fabric of the organization. People make little effort to improve the process; they just live with it the way it is and settle into their part of the work. An organizational change often provides the opportunity not only to improve current processes but also to install new processes that have not yet been defined.

Most significant changes will require some level of process mapping to define and document any changes in processes that are required to enable the new way of working. For example, PAX-Z needs to move from five independent manufacturing sites into one centralized facility in Iowa, so it will need to clarify the manufacturing processes to be used in the new site. Does it just adopt what is currently happening in the Iowa facility? Only if that facility currently has the best processes. Should it build all-new processes? Not if it already has a best practice somewhere in the organization. Every time you make a change, be careful not to toss out what you already have in place. Reuse is a gift, and remember, perfect is the enemy of good enough! If you have something that is good enough, consider using it.

The job requisition process map shown below is a good example of a role-based or "swim-lane" process map. Using this type of process map to clearly define who will touch each task is especially useful for clarifying roles and responsibilities for the execution of the new process. This will help you to avoid battles about who "owns" the work, and by showing how the work will happen differently than it has in the past, you can more easily communicate the "new" way work will happen.

SAMPLE: Basic Process Map

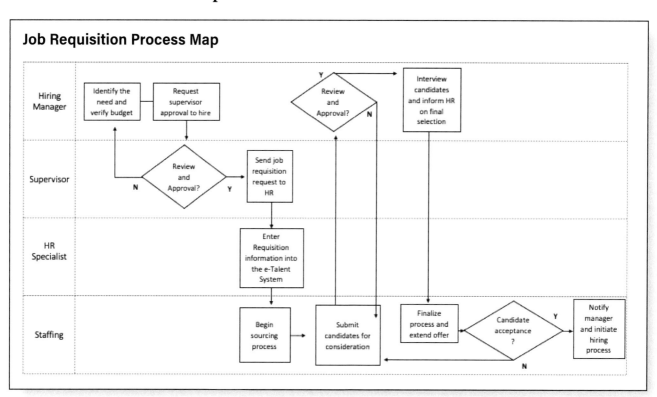

When planning your change, invest the time to determine which processes may need to be reestablished to best support the change. Don't "boil the ocean" and try to reestablish all processes; just focus on those that are core to meeting your change objectives. Separate the *must-have* from the *nice-to-have* process changes, and then take the time necessary to establish, communicate, and ensure accountability for using new processes. If you don't invest time in doing so, employees will continue to use the old process if they can, and it will delay getting traction on your change. Remember: process clarity is a key accelerator.

For more information on process mapping, check out the resources available on our website, or read one of the many books available online on process mapping and cycle-time reduction.

So based on this chapter, here are the common pitfalls to avoid in the "A" or ALIGN component of the MOSAIC framework:

- the inability to accurately identify and actively manage key stakeholders

- a lack of investment in understanding how the change will affect customers and/or impact the daily work of the organization

- the inability to translate broader change objectives down to the individual employee goal plan

- failing to evaluate the level of congruence of existing rewards to the change you are driving (for your change to sustain itself, employees must be rewarded in a way that will move them toward the new way of working)

- failing to identify changes required in policies and practices to sustain your change

- failing to identify, redesign, document, and communicate the process changes required to sustain the change

* * *

The Foundational Tools: Stakeholder Assessment | Work-Impact Analysis | Rewards Assessment | Policy and Practices Assessment | Basic Process Mapping

Chapter 6

Implement Change in a Structured Way

Effective change management requires exceptional project management

In the introduction, I mention two key elements of change management that are missing from traditional OE models. One of those is the *I* in the MOSAIC framework, and it is the topic of this chapter. It's simple. Good change management requires an implementation plan based on strong project management practices.

Years ago a new client asked me to work on a multiyear, multimillion-dollar transformation for one of his business divisions. The president of the business was a great guy, and I liked working with him, but his typical approach to any change project was to name a project manager and then hope that person could somehow get the project over the finish line. Most of us are familiar with the high failure rate that typically results from this 'sink or swim' approach.

After several initial meetings, I approached the CEO with a defined scope of work, estimated timing to complete the project, and an estimate of the cost. After offering me a few colorful expletives, his response was, "We can't afford to have that many people work on this, we can't wait that long to get it done, and we have about half of that budget. What's plan B?" Sound familiar? Perhaps you've even said it yourself or to one of your employees.

Unfortunately the CEO's response was typical of many leaders. They want to accomplish a lot of work with the minimal number of resources in the shortest amount of time. I can't blame them; they are trying to make a profit. Unfortunately that is often the first step toward failure. For any project (including any change project) to be successful, you need to define the right scope of work, appropriately resource and fund that work, and allow the time required to execute it. These three elements—scope, cost, and time—are known by project management professionals as the triple constraints.

The Triple Constraints

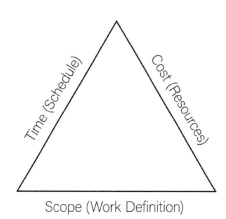

The importance of the triple constraints concept is that all three elements must stay in balance. If you add to the scope of work, you must either extend the timetable to complete that work, or you must fund additional resources. If you need to implement the change sooner, you need to either decrease the scope of work or add resources. And if you need to reduce cost, you need to either decrease the scope of work or extend the timetable to complete the change. This is a simple concept, but it is ignored in 90 percent of the change efforts I have been asked to execute.

There is a reason that 70 percent of change initiatives fail, and ignoring the triple constraints is one of them. Let's talk about why this is so relevant to change management.

Leaders always want more for less, but the reality is that you either pay now or pay later. Do a good job on the front end of the change by investing the time to accurately define the work to be done, investing the appropriate amount of resources required to do the work, and allowing the right amount of time to complete the work, or you'll pay later with a change effort that results in cost overages, delivery delays, and/or critical work being left undone.

When a change is poorly executed, the effort loses momentum and causes organizational fatigue. This results in wasted time, excess cost, and the rather rapid loss of leadership credibility. When you can shorten the time required to execute a change, it saves both time and money. Unfortunately, the sad truth is that most change projects are not well managed, and that contributes to the high failure rate.

Many people invest years to get certified as project managers. Certification includes extensive training, demonstrated multiyear experience in the field as a project manager, successful completion of a certification test, and other requirements. Most project managers are also skilled in the use of project management software, which automates task tracking and reporting. These tools are incredibly useful but, for many smaller companies, too expensive to acquire. As a result, many of the projects I have worked on were planned with a few simple tools and the fairly simple approach to project planning outlined on the following pages. For most of my clients, this simplified, non-tech approach is more than sufficient to manage smaller change projects. It includes the use of seven key tools:

- a project charter to ensure stakeholder alignment

- a basic project plan

- a risk assessment and mitigation plan

- a communication plan to keep all parties informed

- a robust management operating system (MOS) meeting cadence

- a rolling action item list (RAIL) that drives accountability and followup

- a few simple reporting tools to update key stakeholders on project status

Let's look at each of these areas in detail and discuss the tools that support each.

Developing a Project Charter

Think back to a time when you were part of a project planning team—any project planning team. Typically project planning starts with several enthusiastic people sitting around a table talking about the great idea they have for the initiative, project, transformation, et cetera. It often doesn't take long for the team to move from a discussion of the idea to taking action.

One of the key failure modes for many projects (including change projects) is the lack of patience to invest the time necessary to clarify what you are trying to accomplish before you start to act. Successful implementation of any change project requires a good project plan. And a good project plan starts with a clear project charter on what the project is designed to achieve.

I've been asked what the difference is between the plan-on-a-page and a project charter. Here's the answer. In chapter 2, we talked about the plan-on-a-page, which is a simple way to define what you are trying to accomplish as an organization. This tool can be applied at all levels of the organization. The executive level, a work unit, or even an individual can use a plan-on-a-page to focus their effort. It is a broad view of a longer-term plan. Often your strategic outcomes might change slightly over time, but in general, a plan-on-a-page is more enduring; it is a plan that tends to be executed over a longer period. Projects, on the other hand, have clear beginning and end points. Projects are temporary. Projects are a just a slice of the broader plan.

Let's take another look at the sample plan-on-a-page for PAX-Z shown on the following page. As you can see, there are a lot of smaller projects embedded in the priority actions that will need to be accomplished to achieve the overall plan-on-a-page. Each one of these actions (depending on the size of the task) might require a separate project plan to execute the broader plan successfully.

The Plan-on-a-Page for: PAX-Z Golf Company

Mission	Key Strategic Outcomes	Priority Actions	Owner	Due Date
Build affordable, semicustomized clubs and golfing products for recreational golfers to broaden golf's appeal to a wider audience.	1. Realigned and more Focused Portfolio of Products	**1a.** Assess current portfolio of products and make keep/exit recommendations to executive leadership team.	Doris	Feb 17
		1b. Based on approved recommendations (1a), develop project plan to ensure execution by end of year.	**Doris**/Gert	March 13
		1c. Develop an external communication strategy to ensure that partners, customers, vendors, et cetera are aware of changes to our product offerings.	**Doris**/Neal	April 30
		1d. Ensure that manufacturing has changed production processes to align with leadership decisions regarding product offerings.	Fred	May 5
		1e.		
How We Measure Success | KPIs	2. Robust Marketing and Brand Strategy	**2a.** Hire external vendor to conduct a market assessment to define key needs/wants of the recreational market segment.	Doris	Jan 11
		2b. Revise our brand identity to appeal to the recreational market segment.	**Doris**/Sam	April 3
• 24 percent reduction in current product offerings		**2c.** Establish partnerships with schools and golf courses to expand awareness.	**Neal**/Marsha	June 3
		2d. Develop a marketing campaign (including key golf expos) to reintroduce the new PAX-Z to the market.	**Doris**/Sam	April 16
		2e. Work with marketing VP to assess and determine talent requirements for the marketing team.	Doris/**Maggie**	Feb 1
• 15 percent market-share increase in recreational golfing customers within three years	3. Technology Roadmap	**3a.** Partner with marketing to complete a competitive assessment to better understand the technical capabilities of our competition.	Vicki	Feb 9
		3b. Identify key technology needle movers for PAX-Z and associated investment costs.	**Vicki**/Kan	Apr 1
		3c. Recruit two to three engineers with backgrounds in AI engineering, computer science, and physics. Golf experience preferred.	Vicki/**Maggie**	June 4
		3d. Build a three-year technology roadmap to illustrate the availability of new product offerings and associated investment timing.	**Vicki**/Hugh	July 13
		3e.		
• Tech roadmap in place with execution plan defined by end of year	4. Cost-effective Manufacturing	**4a.** Evaluate current manufacturing locations and cost. Make recommendations on how to centralize manufacturing to shorten delivery times and reduce footprint and overall cost.	Fred	April 2
		4b. Complete an assessment of our current supply chain (raw materials availability, supplier quality, etc.) and make recommended changes to improve overall quality and drive cost reduction.	**Fred**/Laura	May 7
		4c. Based on final senior leadership team recommendations, develop final project plan.	Fred	July 10
• Manufacturing capability consolidated by region within eighteen months		**4d.** Based on final approvals, define and document new manufacturing and supply chain processes.	**Fred**/Tommy	Sept 1
		4e.		
		5a.		
		5b.		
		5c.		
		5d.		
		5e.		

For example, to complete priority action 1a, the team will need to "conduct an assessment of the current portfolio of products and services for the company and make keep/exit recommendations to the executive team." Depending on the size of the company and the breadth of the product and service offerings, that task could take anywhere from two days to several months to complete. It is a small project with its own planning requirements and it will require subtasks to complete.

Look at priority action 1b. Once the team has agreed on which product and service offerings to either continue to produce or to stop producing, they will need to build a project plan to execute those decisions. How do you shut down production for product areas that you plan to exit? How will you redeploy employees who currently produce those products? How do you communicate with customers? These types of questions will need to be answered as part of the project plan for this specific priority action. Again, this is a smaller project with its own planning requirements.

Both priority actions mentioned above will require clarity to ensure everyone involved is on the same page in terms of the desired outcomes and the approach to be taken for that priority action. This is where a project charter becomes useful. A project charter is used to clarify and align on the key elements of a project *before* you start building the formal project plan. There are other items you can include here, but basically, a good project charter includes:

- the one-sentence purpose of the project;
- a definition of success criteria for the project;
- a defined sponsor, project leader, and/or project team members;
- which strategic outcome the project supports (this allows managers to avoid having time invested in pet projects that don't support the larger business strategy);
- a list of key stakeholders;
- a definition of what is in and out of scope;
- assumptions (budget availability, resourcing, access to decision makers, timing, etc.);
- preliminary risk factors that should be considered; and
- key milestones/deliverables and expected timing.

As you can see from the PAX-Z example on the following page, Laura Lanny, the project manager assigned to the PAX-Z centralized manufacturing project, has developed a project charter that she will use to negotiate with her managers and other key stakeholders so that she can ensure that everyone is aligned on the desired outcomes *prior* to finalizing her project plan.

Project Charter: Centralized Manufacturing Project

What is the one-sentence purpose of this project?	Consolidate manufacturing capability into our current Iowa factory	Project sponsor (has final approval)	Sam Turner, CEO	Project leader	Laura Lanny, Manager of Equipment and Materials
Which strategic outcome does this project support?	Cost-effective manufacturing	Project team members	• Claudio Smith (finance) • Hugh Budd (engineering) • Petra Quelph (international)		• Tommy Chang (logistics) • Ivan Baranski (HR)
What is in scope for this project?	Review of all current manufacturing facilities and staff Review of all current suppliers	What is out of scope for this project?	• Addition of new and/or upgraded equipment unless approved by Sam • Remapping all current manufacturing processes (stay focused on those related to the move)		
How will we measure the success of this project? Be specific!	Final consolidation occurs within eighteen months No violation of standard production regulations Current production cycle time of less than ten days not negatively impacted through the transition	Who are the key stakeholders for this project?	• Sam Turner, CEO • Fred Jackson, VP of manufacturing • Communities for all our current facilities • Site production employees • Current and/or potential suppliers		
What assumptions should we review with the project sponsor?	The team will have access to Fred and Sam for all scheduled review meetings. Budget and resources will be made available based on final review and approval of the project plan.	What are the two to three key risks we need to consider?	• We are unable to get out of our lease for our Canada facility, which may extend the timeline. • Our most critical production talent will not agree to relocate to the new facility in Iowa.		

What are the key deliverables/milestones? (Preliminary; adjustments made after final project plan is developed)	Owner	Due Date
Manufacturing capability assessment complete	Laura Lanny	April 2
Manufacturing process inventory complete and best practices identified	Laura Lanny	June 16
Material, equipment, WIP, and finished product inventory complete	Mary Monroe	May 7
Risk mitigation plan in place for legal, leases, financial, et cetera	Claudio Smith	May 30
Final project plan completed and approved	Laura Lanny	July 10
Labor management and transition plan complete, including Canadian Works Council	Maggie Madison	Aug. 30
Expansion plan and requirements for Iowa facility finalized and approved	Hugh Budd	Sept. 15
Logistics and transportation and supplier/drayage requirements identified with detailed implementation plan	Tommy Chang	Sept. 1
Employee relations and communication plan in place	Maggie Madison	Nov. 12

Don't underestimate the value of a good project charter. One of the primary benefits of a charter is that it can serve as a negotiating tool between the project leader and management. I once had my manager ask me to "interview thirty of our best leaders and develop a job profile for a what a good general manager should be for our company." It sounded simple enough. I pulled together a small team of four people, and we set off to build a project plan. It wasn't a big plan. It had only 162 tasks. In the end the team decided that it would take $5,700 to pay a consultant to help aggregate all the data we would collect, and we thought we could complete the project in less than ten weeks. It wasn't until I brought the plan to my manager for review that I discovered that his view was that we had "no funding for consultants, and we need it done in three weeks." Although the rigor of our project plan ultimately changed his mind, I could have avoided the conflict entirely if I had completed and reviewed a project charter (which would have included the assumptions I was making about available budget and timing) before we finalized the project plan. This would have given me an opportunity to clarify his expectations and to better understand the boundaries before I pulled the team together.

Laura's ability to complete her charter enabled her to confirm timing of deliverables, assumptions about resources, budget, et cetera and negotiate what she needed for the project to be successful *before* she started executing a plan.

Developing a Basic Project Plan

People often ask me if they should buy project management software to plan their change. Although that can be incredibly helpful, especially for a large project, software won't help you if you don't understand the basic elements of project management. For most change projects, it has been my experience that you can develop a fairly robust project plan with a large wall and some stickies. You can find additional step-by-step instructions on how to run your low-tech project plan meeting from the learning modules on our website, but the information below is a high-level overview of the basic process that we have used for years with clients who can't afford to buy software. Let's start with some basics on how to think about project planning.

Once you have an agreed-upon charter, you must complete a scope of work. The scope of work is basically a list of all the tasks that need to be completed to achieve the change. The team brainstorms all the various actions that must occur to successfully implement the project. Again, each task should start with a verb. *Verbs matter!* As mentioned earlier, there is a big difference between "develop a strategy" (which could take two hours) and "implement the strategy" (which could take two years). Each of the small blue lines below represents a task that is required to execute the change.

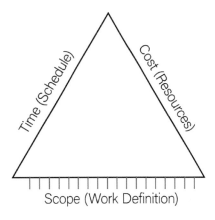

The scope of work serves as the foundation for all the additional planning. Typically, once you have brainstormed all the tasks required to successfully implement the project, the individual tasks are grouped into buckets of like work. For example, when building her project plan, Laura Lanny had a dozen tasks that were all related to the inventory of existing manufacturing processes. These tasks could all be grouped under a key deliverable or milestone called "Manufacturing process inventory complete and best practices identified." This bucket became one of the key deliverables on her charter. Once your tasks are grouped into key deliverables (or milestones), sort the deliverables into a sequence. Which one needs to happen first? Which needs to happen second? Et cetera. (If they can happen concurrently, just place them side by side.) Once you have sequenced the deliverables, then proceed to sequence the tasks and subtasks associated with each deliverable.

Your scope should include anything that consumes resources, including project meetings, client meetings, et cetera. The more detailed the list, the more accurate your final plan will be. That being said, too much detail can be paralyzing, so strike a good balance between enough scope definition to build a good plan, estimated costs, and a completion timeline, but not getting so buried in detail you don't have time to actually execute the plan.

Once you have identified all the required tasks, review each element of the scope of work and document how long it will take to complete each listed task. For example, it may take two hours to develop your customer satisfaction survey, but it will probably take several days to summarize all the data into the consolidated report. You would repeat this for every task identified as part of your scope of work. This is known in project management as defining *duration* for the tasks. Each of the red lines below represents the time required to complete each task.

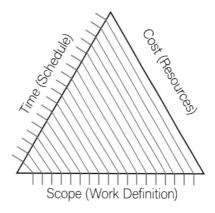

When you calculate durations, do not include what's known as "lag" or "lead" time. For example, "Develop the survey" may be a task that takes a total of six hours. But you may have to wait two weeks to allow customers time to respond to the survey. It is important to identify only the six hours as your duration because that is an accurate reflection of the time it will take to develop the survey. This is needed to identify the resources required to accomplish the task. You would not include the two-week waiting or lag time, because waiting may affect your end date, but it doesn't require resources. Similarly, to distribute your survey, you may have a task that reads, "Obtain customer mailing list information." It may take you fifteen minutes to call another department and request the mailing list. However, you may have to wait a week for the department to assemble and send the mailing list before you can distribute your survey. This delay in receiving the list is known as lead time. Like lag time, you do not include it in your duration. Both lead time and lag time are reflected in your final calendar, not in the actual time consumed by the tasks. (By the way, any task that takes less than an hour is generally reflected as a full hour on your plan just to keep things simple.) Once you add up all the durations and add any necessary delays, you'll get a sense of how long the project will take.

Once you've identified the scope of work by identifying each task and how long each task will take (duration), you will need to identify any dependencies. For example, Laura's plan for PAX-Z centralized manufacturing will require her to shut down existing facilities. However, her ability to do so is dependent on having the new facility completed. Therefore one task is dependent on another. Shutting down existing production facilities should not be scheduled prior to the opening of the new facility. These dependencies must be reflected in your schedule to accurately determine how long the entire project will take.

To develop an estimated timeline, make a calendar on the wall and then group your key deliverables and subtasks in sequence according to the duration you have defined for each task. Be sure to reflect lead and lag times in the schedule. You will also want to look for opportunities to shorten your overall timeline by pulling in work that can happen concurrently. For example, at the end of the centralized manufacturing project, Laura will want to conduct an evaluation of how effectively the new centralized manufacturing facility is working. Even though she will not launch that evaluation for eighteen months, she can design it now. She can be doing that work at the beginning of the project because it is not dependent on any other tasks. By doing this, she will shorten her overall time to complete the project.

Finally, you'll need to assign resources and/or cost to each task. These are represented as the green lines below.

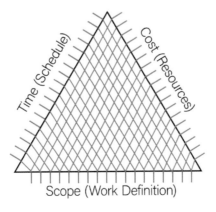

There are two types of cost estimates. "Top-down" is an estimate based on past projects. A "bottom-up" estimate is more accurate. To establish a "bottom-up" cost estimate, you would need to look at every task and determine any cost associated with that task. For example, "Obtain customer mailing list" may have a fee associated with the purchase of the list. That cost would be assigned to that task. Once you add them all up, you'll have a general idea of what your project will cost. Professional project managers will go into the detail of calculating salaries, percentages of resources, et cetera. Again, to keep it simple, it probably wouldn't be worthwhile to do that unless you were charging costs back to an external customer. However, if you are using resources outside your organization, make sure to include that in your overall cost estimate.

I have seen a wide variety of project plans that are used to document the work to be done, identify the cost of that work, develop a timetable for completion of the project, calculate the overall cost, assign responsibility for the work, and then monitor progress against the plan. Again, software programs are wonderful for managing your project if you can afford them. If you are unable to purchase software, for most projects, a simple Microsoft Excel tool can suffice. As you can see from the PAX-Z project plan on the next page, the important thing is to have a method of documenting the work to be done and have the ability to update the status of the actions so that the project manager can easily identify if the project is on or off track. This is essential when attempting to monitor your progress. More about monitoring later in this chapter.

This chapter will also find us reviewing additional planning tools for risk mitigation, communication, et cetera. It is important to migrate action plans from those tools into your overall project plan to enable one source of truth for the work that needs to get done.

Basic Project Plan: PAX-Z Centralized Manufacturing

PAX-Z Centralized Manufacturing Project Plan

Status	
Not Started	
Immediate Action Required	
Active w/Concerns	
Active & On Track	
Complete	

DELIVERABLE/ MILESTONE	Task #	Task Description	Duration (hours)	Dependent on Another Task? If So, List Task #	Start Date	Scheduled Due Date	Owner	Status R/Y/G/B	If behind Schedule, Please Comment
1. Current manufacturing-capability assessment completed, including evaluation of regulatory requirements	1.1	Prepare list of major capital assets and assess condition, value, et cetera	8		1-Jan	2-Apr	Fred		Resource challenges being addressed
	1.2	Identify and review all planned CapEx investments	4		1-Jan	2-Apr	Fred		
	1.3	Review contracts	4		1-Jan	2-Apr	Fred		
	1.4	Reassess contracts based on potentially revised manufacturing strategies	6		1-Jan	2-Apr	Fred		
	1.5	Exchange/synch equipment standardization guidelines	3		1-Jan	2-Apr	Fred		
	1.6	Create new capital plan	6	1.1, 1.2, 6.1	1-Jan	2-Apr	Claudio		Dependencies
2. Material, equipment, WIP, and finished product inventory complete	2.1	Understand the current inventory profile and key drivers	2		1-Apr	7-May	Tommy		
	2.2	Prepare storage plans for material and equipment to be shipped to Iowa	4		1-Apr	7-May	Tommy		
	2.3	Complete WIP production and ship to customers	40		15-Jul	30-Aug	Mary		
	2.4								
	2.5								
	2.6								
3. Risk-mitigation plan in place for legal, leases, financial, et cetera	3.1	Identify and classify risks associated with centralizing manufacturing	2		15-Jan	1-Feb	Fred		
	3.2	Prepare mitigation strategies for all high-risk factors	2		15-Jan	1-Feb	Fred		
	3.3	Add risk review to scheduled project updates	0.5		15-Jan	1-Feb	Fred		
	3.4								
	3.5								
	3.6								
4. Final project plan completed and approved	4.1	Consolidate and upload detailed task list to Excel	1		1-Jan	30-Jun	Fred		Project team members delayed in sending their list
	4.2	Review and finalize project plan	1	4.1	1-Jan	10-Jul	Fred		Pending receipt of task lists
	4.3	Schedule project plan review with senior leadership team	0.5		15-Jan	13-Jul	Fred		
	4.4	Communicate to all employees upon final approval	0.5	8.2,		15-Jul	Sam		
	4.5								
	4.6								
5. Labor management and transition plan complete	5.1	Schedule and hold initial meeting with Canadian Works Council	4		1-May	1-Jun	Maggie		Scheduling conflicts; working to resolve
	5.2	Reach agreement on site-closure process	2	5.1	1-May	30-Aug	Maggie		Pending meeting with Canadian Works Council
	5.3	Communicate with impacted employees on severance packages	8	8.2	1-Sep	15-Sep	Maggie		
	5.4	Retain outside legal counsel (labor expertise)	1		15-Apr	15-May	Maggie		
	5.5	Assess training needs and provide options for skill upgrades	16		1-Jun	30-Jul	Maggie		
	5.6								
	6.1	Assess Iowa site for expanded production capability	8		1-Jan	15-Mar	Fred		

Remember, good change management requires a good project plan. When change projects fail, the failure is seldom attributed to management. Instead, the project leader tends to get blamed for the failure. By understanding how to build a robust project plan and more effectively work with your sponsor to manage the triple constraints through execution, you increase the likelihood of a successful change effort. (And you keep your job!)

Finally, it's worth mentioning that you can go very deep in project planning, or you can stay high level. It really depends on your needs. Most of my clients are happy to develop a basic plan that describes the work to be done and gives them a general idea of cost and timing. For more extensive training on project management, buy a copy of the *Project Management Body of Knowledge* (*PMBOK*), which is the main study guide for PMI certification.

Risk Assessment

Part of any project planning for your organizational change should include a quick assessment of the risks you could face when implementing your change and a list of the key actions to be taken to mitigate those risks. This is a simple thirty-minute exercise, so don't overcomplicate it. Often when you get a team together to do this, they attempt to document all the risks for current pain points in the organization. However, it is important to keep in mind that the focus of this exercise should include *only those risks associated with the implementation of your change.* The result should be a list of specific risks you will likely face during implementation. Once you have defined the potential risks, focus your energy on those things that are high risk and most likely to happen. Once you have identified key actions, transfer those actions to your project plan so that you can ensure that your mitigation plan is in place. Here is a sample risk assessment from the PAX-Z Centralized Manufacturing project.

Risk Assessment: Centralized Manufacturing

What Could Go Wrong During the Change Process?	Risk Level (L, M, H)	What Should Be Done to Lessen the Risk? (Include This in Your Project Plan or RAIL)	Who Should Do It?	Due Date
Production equipment breaks during move to Iowa plant	H	• Produce a schedule to include required contractors; contact them well in advance • Prepare layout drawings and audit machinery and equipment • Plan and communicate changes to supply chain employees • Create and distribute work instructions	Fred Jackson	Aug. 1
Canadian union employees stage a strike	L	• Comply with employee protection laws • Communicate with union representatives regularly • Engage employees in the change process and ask for input	Maggie/ Petra	Ongoing
Supplier negotiations take longer than expected	M	• Communicate up front with suppliers • Show continued loyalty by reaching out to suppliers weekly • Pay suppliers on time per contractual obligations	Tommy Chang	March 30
Employee morale declines	M	• Practice transparency and empathy by holding weekly meetings • Provide recognition to employees that display support for the change • Collect feedback from focus groups and put an action plan in place to respond	Ivan/ Maggie	Ongoing
Key leaders resign	L	• Identify leaders at risk of leaving and invite Sam to have a 1:1 conversation with each • Consider potential retention agreements for at-risk talent • Have a backup plan in place should a resignation occur	Sam/ Maggie	Jan. 30

Remember the key concept behind the MOSAIC approach—an organization is an integrated system, so your change approach must consider the whole, not just the parts, of the system. Risk mitigation provides the opportunity to anticipate and plan for potential unintended consequences of implementing your change. The new way of doing things may add value, but you will need to anticipate and plan for any negative, unintended consequences.

Communication Planning

Nido R. Qubein, the president of High Point University, once said, "The organization that can't communicate can't change, and the corporation that can't change is dead." He couldn't be more accurate. When implementing small changes, leaders can often just announce the change, and it will happen. For example, "Here is our new company logo; start using it." It doesn't really change much in an employee's daily life, and very little effort is required on the part of the employee to support the implementation of a new logo. However, significant and potentially disruptive change requires consistent, two-way communication. In these situations leaders need to listen much more than they talk, especially in the early stages of the change. The communication plan template on the following page is a method of documenting the key communication objectives and key messages for those most impacted by your change.

Generally, the targets of your communication plan are the stakeholders that you have identified as those necessary to involve or consult based on Mendelow's matrix that we discussed in chapter 5. As you can see from the PAX-Z example below, the project team has identified key stakeholders and developed specific actions to be taken to ensure a good balance of both downward communication and upward feedback. This allows them to send out the right messages while ensuring they fully understand the challenges from the employees' perspective. This is an effective and necessary approach when implementing disruptive change.

Communication Plan: Centralized Manufacturing

Audience/ Stakeholder	Key Objectives/Messages	Preferred Method	Frequency	Owner
All Global PAX-Z Employees	• Company plan-on-a-page, business case for centralized manufacturing, timeline, project leader, and how to escalate issues/concerns • Keep them informed, FAQs, feedback to us—provide opportunities for upward feedback on issues/concerns	Town halls and employee portal updates	Quarterly 24/7	**Laura** Lanny Gert Glendon
Manufacturing Site Employees	• Keep them informed—project progress, what's new, their role, expectations, et cetera • Site check-in sessions—gather feedback/issues/concerns	Face-to-face meetings at each site	Every quarter though transition	**Laura/** Maggie
Suppliers	• The overall plan, timeline, and project leader; impact on current contracts; who to contact with concerns	Virtual—video call / teleconference	Monthly	Laura Lanny
Key Customers	• All customers: "we are not shutting down business, just moving facilities to better serve you." • Impacted customers: portfolio changes / implications / upsell	1:1 calls (for impacted customers)	Monthly	Marsha Phillips
Canadian Workers Union Reps	• Works Council meeting updates, investment in new Canadian research facility, how to escalate issues/concerns	Virtual—video call / teleconference	As required	**Maggie** and external labor counsel

Management Operating System

A management operating system, or MOS, as it is often called, is the set of tools, meetings, and behaviors a leader uses to manage people and processes to deliver business results. I have yet to meet a client who was able to successfully implement a significant change in the absence of a strong MOS. More than any other alignment factor, your ability to establish a strong meeting cadence will ensure an ongoing push to drive your change forward. It is the ultimate MOSAIC "glue." In simple terms, your meeting cadence should:

• establish a meeting cadence across the organization that allows the right people to discuss the right things at the right time;

- provide opportunities for the escalation and resolution of key obstacles to progress on the change;

- enable actions to be assigned so that you can ensure accountability; and

- establish a reporting process so that you can monitor progress and have ongoing visibility into how well the organization is working together to accomplish the plan.

I once worked with a very obsessive-compulsive CEO. Each year at the end of November, he would have his administrative assistant go into the calendar system and put hundreds of meetings on the calendar for the coming year. And I mean hundreds. Our calendars were overwhelmed before the year even started. Looking back on that, I came to appreciate the rigor with which he drove the organization. I was forced to work around his series of very structured meetings. However, if I wanted to bring a concern forward, I knew exactly in which meeting I should bring it up. He made it easy for me to plug into key discussions because I always knew when the meeting would be held and exactly who would be there. Additionally, he started every monthly staff meeting with a quick review of assigned actions, and everyone knew that it was career suicide to show up and announce that you hadn't made progress on your assignments. His discipline drove a rigor of accountability that ensured forward movement, and I came to truly appreciate the value that added to our ability to drive change.

Over the years I have found three simple tools that will help you drive a more efficient operating system: the MOS meeting cadence, a rolling action-item list (RAIL), and simple but informative reporting tools. Let's talk about each of them.

Meeting Cadence

Every leader should have an established cadence to identify the various meetings that need to be held to ensure that the right conversations are occurring with the appropriate people within the appropriate time frame. If you don't have a general meeting cadence for your organization, you can use the form on the following page to establish one. See the next page for the general meeting cadence for the PAX-Z executive team. Note that while not specific to a change project, the centralized manufacturing project update is included as an agenda topic in the monthly executive team staff meeting.

Meeting Cadence: PAX-Z Executive Team

What is the name of the meeting?	What needs to be discussed? Be specific!	How often does it happen, and how long does it last?	Who should attend?	Who sets it up?
Monthly Executive Team Staff Meeting	• RAIL review • Financial/business update, sales pipeline review, customer review and key actions, review of pending HR issues, review of alignment on our service-level agreements—are they working as planned?	Monthly—two hours	All direct reports	Sam
Monthly 1:1s with Sam	• Monthly one-on-one update meetings with each staff member and Sam. Use the monthly goal update (three-up provided) • Highlight any topics that require his visibility (heads-up)	Monthly—one hour	Sam and the direct report	Direct report to get it on the calendar
Quarterly All-Hands Meeting	PAX-Z business update from Sam, quarterly customer updates, progress on key initiatives, quarterly rewards and recognition	Quarterly—one hour for all PAX-Z employees	All PAX-Z employees	Sam
Annual Strategic Planning	Review and develop the strategic plan—strategic forecasting	Q3 every year	Executive team and key members of marketing	Doris Chen
Biannual Talent Review Meeting	Strategic talent review and calibration: What is our talent capability? Where are we strong or not strong? Where is our top talent? Who is having performance issues? What is the "get well" plan? This is an organizational health check.	March and September of each year	Executive team	Maggie
Special Project Update—Centralizing Manufacturing	Project status and any red (behind-schedule) items, resource requirements, issues, obstacles, or help needed	Weekly—one hour with all executive team members	Executive team without Sam	Laura Lanny—project leader
What meetings will we stop doing?	• Multisite review meetings (once we have centralized manufacturing in place)			

When establishing your meeting schedule for your change project, you can either fit your change into an existing meeting cadence or establish your own. If your organization already provides the right meeting opportunities to communicate to the right people, and enough time to discuss and resolve obstacles, then add your change as one of the agenda topics. If not, establish a new meeting cadence that better meets your needs. For most of my larger change projects, I tend to build a hybrid. I insert leadership reviews and updates into an existing meeting cadence (such as adding the change as an agenda item on the leadership staff meeting) and then establish my own project team meeting schedule with a singular focus on the change effort.

A strong meeting cadence needs to support the execution of your strategic plan. Once you have done your annual planning, review your meeting cadence. Ask yourself, "What meetings need to be added? What meetings need to be deleted? What agenda items need to be added/eliminated?" Don't build a meeting cadence once and then use the same schedule into perpetuity. If you don't regularly review the appropriateness of your meeting cadence, you'll end up adding meetings but never removing any, and then people spend more time in meetings and less time serving your customers.

The Rolling Action-Item List (RAIL)

A rolling action-item list, or RAIL, is a common tool for leaders to manage accountability and follow-up for their teams. A RAIL is a list of all action items, when they are due, the person responsible for the action, and the status of the action at the time it is reported.

The RAIL below illustrates how Sam, the CEO of PAX-Z, tracks actions for his team. As you saw in the PAX-Z meeting cadence shown on the prior page, each monthly staff meeting starts with a RAIL review. This is a rapid-fire review of status on the actions. New actions are added to the RAIL each month during the executive leadership team meetings. Let's take a deeper look at how to develop and most effectively use a RAIL.

Rolling Action Item List: Executive Team

Status
Not Started
Immediate Action Required
Active w/Concerns
Active & On Track
Complete

Action - Must include a verb!	Assigned to	Due Date	Status	Comments
Develop a reward and incentive system targeted toward innovation activity	Maggie	30-Sep		
Establish a list of key processes and set up cross-functional teams to map and define best practices in manufacturing	Fred	2-Jan		
Define short- and long-term capital expenditure plan	Claudio	4-Apr		
Revise our current pricing strategy for margin-improvement opportunities	Neal	31-Jul		
Develop a strong, simplified, standardized budgeting process and tools	Claudio	28-May		Need to replace external vendor we were working with, so timeline delayed slightly
Identify clear gaps in our PAX-Z product portfolio and recommend build, buy, or partner actions	**Doris** with Neal	30-Jun		
Implement an organization and talent review process, including an approach to the identification of top talent and structured succession planning	Maggie	18-Mar		
Develop data strategy and dashboard to track/measure talent development progress	Maggie	1-Oct		Waiting on Vicki to finalize platform
Establish a process to ensure that we can monitor the trends in discounts across the sales team to ensure guidelines are consistent across the customer base	Neal	7-Jul		

A RAIL is often built in Excel to allow a leader to sort tasks based on multiple factors. With the increased availability of online systems, you can also create a multitude of virtual RAILs. Whatever tool you choose to use, make it a habit. If a RAIL review isn't a habitual, disciplined process for your team, you will never capitalize on the opportunity to improve your organization's performance by ensuring follow-up and accountability on key actions.

The use of a RAIL can become just another piece of bureaucracy if it isn't managed well. The guidance on the following pages can help you successfully implement a RAIL process.

Completing the RAIL Input

- Every RAIL action needs a verb and a clear statement of the action to be taken. Posting a RAIL action that says "Fix our quality issues" is useless. How would you measure that? How would I know when the action was complete? A better action would be something like, "Meet with customer XYZ, define the quality issue he is facing, and ensure a plan is in place to address his current issue and resolve the root cause." When posting any action to a RAIL, the action must be specific and measurable.

- Each action needs a clear, targeted due date. Don't put "July" into a RAIL action; put a realistic but actual date. If you miss the deadline, you can modify as needed, but have a clear starting point.

- Every RAIL action needs one clear owner for the action. A good rule to follow is this: "If everyone is accountable, then no one is accountable." Can you have a team work on an action? Absolutely. But you need to start with a single person who has ownership to get the action over the finish line. As you can see on the sample PAX-Z RAIL on the prior page, if you want to identify multiple people to participate, list all the names but bold the name of the person who will lead the action forward. As you can see on row 6, Doris and Neal share the action, but Doris is bolded, so she is on point to lead.

Use good judgment on what needs to go into the RAIL. Each team must choose a comfortable level of input when completing a RAIL, but my suggestion is to not overload your RAIL with minutia. Don't waste time tracking small pieces of work that will happen just as a natural course of doing business. For example, if I know that we will have a standing sales review meeting, I don't need to record that we need a standing sales review meeting—it will happen without me tracking it.

Conducting a RAIL Review

- A leader needs to actively sponsor the use of a RAIL. If you don't actively use it with your team, it will be a waste of everyone's time, so show up and model the appropriate use of the tool.

- Establish and communicate a process to allow team members to provide status on their individual action items *prior* to the RAIL review. Where can you centrally locate the file so that everyone can easily add their status? When does status input need to be completed?

- If the status is updated, a RAIL review is a five- to ten-minute exercise. If, however, the team members fail to update the status prior to the meeting, you will waste a lot of time discussing each item. Therefore, it is important that the leader hold the team accountable for completing the status input prior to the RAIL review. Once all input has been posted, the meeting leader sorts the RAIL by status and due date. Common status categories are shown below.

- Not started (white)

- Immediate action required (red)

- Active with concerns (yellow)

- Active and on track (green)

- Complete (blue)

- Just like good project management reviews, a RAIL process is best managed *by exception*. Any item that is green or yellow is assumed to be on track and/or at a manageable level of risk. Therefore, only red or past-due items are reviewed.

- Once the RAIL is sorted, the leader guides a quick discussion of each red or past-due action item. The goal of the review discussion is to ask the action owner for one sentence as to why the action is at risk and/or delayed.

- *Do not attempt to solve the problem during the meeting!* Identify the key obstacles and then quickly decide on the best next step. Should you extend the due date? Should another action be added? Should another resource get involved?

- After the review, move any completed (blue) actions to the completed-action worksheet.

I'm often asked, "What is the difference between a standard project plan (which includes tasks to be completed) and a RAIL document?" Great question. Projects should have a clear beginning and a clear end date. A project may last two months, two years, et cetera. But the key thing to keep in mind about a project is that it is temporary. The actions on a project plan are specific to that project, and the project plan is used to track only those actions that are specific to *that* project. A project plan is only useful during the life of the project.

A RAIL document is enduring. Leaders use a RAIL document on an ongoing basis to document and track key actions to be taken by their team. Do not put all your project plan actions into your RAIL, or your RAIL review will become a nightmare to manage. It is better to set up and conduct separate project reviews to track the status of actions for a specific project. Project update charts (UP charts) are a great way to get a quick status report on a project without reviewing every single task item on the project plan.

Reporting UP Charts

To monitor the status of a change project, I generally sort my project plan by status (just like the RAIL) and then focus on any at-risk and/or past-due actions on the plan. However, when meeting with executive teams to provide updates, this is a laborious process and opens the door to conversations that distract from your primary two-pronged objective: provide a status update to leadership and get help to resolve any obstacles to successfully implementing the change. To best serve that purpose, you might want to consider a simpler form of reporting.

One of the best things Jeff Bezos did as the leader of Amazon was to ban PowerPoint from meetings. Instead he insisted that participants silently read a hard-copy document containing the information necessary to discuss the issue. Good for him! Spending hour after hour pouring over PowerPoint slides is one of the most draining exercises in business today. The average executive spends 50 percent of their time in meetings. Unfortunately, subordinates trying to impress the boss have turned making perfect slides into an art form that appears to have replaced high-quality conversations.

I must confess I have not been able to eliminate the use of slide decks, but I am (like most people) a visual person. I like having something to look at to launch a discussion—it grounds me. It can quickly bring everyone to the same baseline understanding of what is going on so that we can zero in on the key items that we need to discuss. So how do you quickly get meeting participants up to speed on an issue so you can focus on the discussion instead of wading through slides? With that goal in mind, I am a big advocate of using UP charts to quickly convey information.

In printing lingo, terms like *four-up*, *three-up*, and *two-up* refer to the way printing plates and/or artwork files are designed to allow the printing press to apply more than one image to the paper at the same time. A four-up format creates four images per press impression, a three-up format creates three images per press impression, and so on.

As you can see from the sample UP charts on the following pages, an UP-chart template is a tool that can quickly baseline a group's understanding so you can focus on the conversation, not the charts. I've included two different samples.

Individual Goals Update

The three-up chart on the next page is an example of a tool that is commonly used by leaders to quickly get an update on the progress employees are making on their individual goals. It is equally useful for a project manager to quickly obtain a status report from each member of the change team. When implementing larger changes, I ask each project team member to complete this document regularly and post it to a shared site that is accessible to all members of the change team. This allows the team to stay informed on what other team members have accomplished in the last thirty days, what they are working on for the next thirty days, and what issues we may be facing so we can work together to resolve them.

If you decide to use this form with your change project team, remind the team that this is not intended as an exhaustive list of all they are doing. The goal is to hit the highlights to keep everyone informed.

Individual Goals Update: Claudio Smith   Revised: Sept. 7

Accomplishments in the Last Thirty Days

- Disposition of unsold PAX Pro 105 apparel completed
- Presented initial financial outlook to PAX-Z board
- Completed all quarterly staff performance reviews
- Fiscal year books closed—favorable report on external audit

Upcoming in the Next Thirty Days

- Complete three-year financial outlook for review by board
- Prepare six-month budget outlook and complete final review with Sam
- Review online invoicing tool with Laura Lanny and present recommendations to executive team
- Complete first draft of capital expenditure proposal

Key Issues/Risks and Actions Needed

Issue/Risk	Action Needed	Owner	Due Date
Potential delay in capital expenditure draft for Iowa	Input on capital equipment needs. Need final details on Canada plant closure timing as soon as available.	Fred Jackson	Nov. 12

Project Update

When providing updates to your management on how your change project is progressing, the standard four-up chart shown on the next page can allow you to keep the executive team and/or key stakeholders focused on the key messages you are trying to convey (i.e., what progress have we made, what obstacles are we facing that we need help to resolve, et cetera.) In this example, Laura Lanny is showing the specific accomplishments, upcoming work, overall status against the key milestones, and surfacing two obstacles that need to be discussed.

Project Update: Centralized Manufacturing Project

Leader Name: Laura Lanny
Updated on: March 4

Accomplishments in the Last Thirty Days

- Project team in place, first working session held
- Completed employee town hall to announce project and take questions
- Completed initial best practices evaluation of current manufacturing processes
- Finished project evaluation survey and process

Upcoming in the Next Thirty Days

- Subteams launched and working sessions scheduled
- Interview and retain external counsel—Canadian Works Council issues
- Conduct first site focus groups

Project Milestone Status

Milestone	Status
Current manufacturing capability assessment completed, including evaluation of regulatory requirements	
Material, equipment, WIP, and finished product inventory complete	
Risk mitigation plan in place for legal, leases, financial, et cetera	
Final project plan completed and approved	
Labor management and transition plan complete	
Expanded plan and requirements for Iowa facility finalized and approved	
Logistics, transportation, and supplier/drayage requirements identified with detailed implementation plan	
Employee relations and communication plan in place	

Key Issues/Risks and Help Needed

Issue/Risk	Owner	Due Date
Potential delay in capital expenditure draft for Iowa due to Canada plant closure timing details	Fred Jackson	TBD
Need another representative from sales to join the change team so we better understand the impact on customers	Neal	End of month

☐ Not started ■ Immediate action required ■ Active with concerns ■ Active and on track ■ Complete

Any reporting tools need to respond to what matters most to your management team and key stakeholders. Personally, I believe that simple templates such as UP charts prevent unnecessary distractions resulting from too much data and they serve to focus the conversation where you need it. However, after you have completed your initial project charter, it is important to clarify reporting expectations. Clarify how often management wants to meet to discuss the change. What do they most want to discuss? Being clear on those expectations can go a long way toward obtaining the support you will need to drive your change.

Whatever structure or tools you use to conduct your change project review meeting, run the review meetings efficiently. Have a clear agenda. Start and stop on time. It is important to establish rigor around the review meetings. Changes have a way of getting pushed aside when you have a business or organization to run. A consistent drumbeat with key leaders about the progress of the change effort keeps it front and center with the organization. It also provides a venue for you to deal with issues arising from the five fatal flaws discussed in the next chapter.

Summary

So based on this chapter, here are the common pitfalls to avoid in the "I" or IMPLEMENT component of the MOSAIC framework:

- not clarifying the project requirements prior to executing the change

- failing to manage the change just as you would any other big project

- not assessing your implementation risks and developing adequate mitigation plans

- not establishing effective two-way communication

- not establishing an effective management operating system (MOS) that creates the push the change requires (a strong meeting cadence, accountability, monitoring, and reporting)

* * *

The Foundational Tools: Project Charter | Basic Project Plan | Risk Assessment | Communication Plan | Meeting Cadence | Rolling Action-Item List (RAIL) | Reporting UP Charts

Chapter 7

Change Principles—the Five Fatal Flaws

If you fail to abide by the key change principles, your change will fail!

Many times, I get called in after a change has gone sideways, which makes recovery even harder. We've talked about the significant percentage (70 percent) of changes that fail to take hold in an organization. Most of us have had the experience of watching a change that is launched with good intentions and then quickly abandoned as leaders leave the organization or move to new roles. This lack of traction and the inability to ensure the "stickiness" of the change can often be attributed to what I'll call the five fatal flaws. There are certainly other factors that can impede a change, but it has been my experience that the five principles outlined on the following pages are the key contributors to failed change activity.

Bookshelves are loaded with books on leadership. In this chapter I don't want to focus on basic leadership principles. Instead I want to focus specifically on the behaviors (predominantly practiced by leaders) that significantly contribute to either the success or the failure of change. To sustain a change effectively, leaders at all levels of the organization should understand and practice these behaviors until they become habitual. Avoiding the five fatal flaws is essential to implementing and sustaining a change.

Fatal Flaw #1—Ineffective Sponsorship

Our first fatal flaw is the inability to engage in the behaviors that demonstrate strong sponsorship for the change. This includes a lack of visible support, failure to abide by the triple constraints, the inability to ensure that employees feel accountable for the change, and marginalizing the change objectives to keep everyone happy.

Demonstrate Visible Support

This is not a hard thing to do, but most leaders fail to invest the time to do it. Generally leaders will delegate responsibility for the change effort to a subordinate and then expect that person to be able to control the behaviors of others, who may or may not be a part of their organization. That is unfair to the employee and sends a message to the organization that the leader doesn't care enough to be personally involved. If employees don't see the leader personally invest time in the change, they won't think that the change matters enough for them to invest time either. Therefore, when a leader announces a new initiative or change, it needs to be accompanied by active involvement in the change process. My message to leaders who want to ensure the changes happen is, "Don't sit in the stadium watching the race; get on the field and run." I am not implying that the leader does all the implementation work; the project change team can do that. What I am saying is that they need to send a clear message to the organization that "I want this to be successful, and I expect you to support it."

Abide by the Triple Constraints

An effective sponsor provides adequate resources and funding to support the triple constraints of good project management (see chapter 6). Define the scope of work to effectively implement the change, establish a realistic timetable, and then resource the change appropriately. It's basic: partial resourcing will give you partial results.

Drive Accountability for Success

Leaders must ensure that employees clearly understand that behaviors in support of the change will be rewarded and that there will consequences for not supporting the change. For example, if we install a new process for paying invoices, employees must be held accountable for using the new invoicing process. It sounds simple, doesn't it? Unfortunately many leaders underestimate the significance of their role in dealing with unsupportive behaviors and thus take a soft approach to dissension. Let me give you an example.

Ralph was the CEO of a billion-dollar organization. In fifteen years, the business had grown from a small group of less than 100 people in a single city to a 4,800-person organization across the globe. It had made multiple acquisitions but never integrated any of them, so every process was done differently in every office across the globe. Like many other organizations, it had continued to add cost structure that now limited its ability to scale. To reposition the organization for growth, this organization needed to reset its business strategy, implement a structured portfolio management process to ensure its product and service offerings were aligned with the marketplace, evaluate its organizational structure, and conduct a reduction in force, which was something it had never experienced in the history of the company. Additionally, it needed to evaluate and adjust its global footprint—the bricks and mortar of the organization. In some cases it had five small offices of less than 10 people in the same city within a mile of each other. It was a prolonged and painful process and not to be undertaken by the faint of heart. It was clear what needed to be done; the board of directors knew it, and so did Ralph.

Unfortunately Ralph had a member of his staff named Peter. Peter had been in his role for twenty-seven years and was making $2.5 million a year as the head of one of the business divisions. Over time he had hired a team that did most of his work for him. It was clear to everyone in the organization that if you worked for Peter, you would do the work, and in turn, he would let you do what you wanted. That was the unspoken understanding. The changes that Ralph wanted to make would completely upset Peter's comfortable life of not having to do much and still make a lot of money—he might actually have to work for a change, and he had no intention of investing any time or energy in changing anything this late in his career. Peter would openly criticize what Ralph was trying to do. When his team would push back in staff meetings, he would be heard saying, "Don't worry. It will never happen; I won't let it." His active sabotage of the change effort sent ripples of resistance through the organization.

Ralph and Peter had been colleagues since the organization was founded—and they were close friends. Ralph's inability to hold Peter (and others) accountable delayed implementation of much-needed changes and sent a message to the organization that if you chose not to implement the change, there would be no consequence for doing so, and as a result, Ralph's credibility with the organization plummeted. People just stopped listening to his messages about the change because they no longer believed that he was serious about it. If he didn't care enough to hold his own team accountable, why should they?

In these situations, leaders need to act quickly. Set up a private meeting with the employee to offer them one more opportunity to identify any additional obstacles. If it is clearly just one more excuse as to why the employee won't get on board, then the leader must make it clear that the employee must support the change. I often hear the argument, "Well, the employee might leave if we force them to get on board." In those situations the leader should ask themselves, "Do I really want an employee who refuses to support something we need to do?" The answer, of course, is no. It is essential that leaders confront behavior that is not supportive of the new way of doing things. When employees (without good reason) are either publicly or privately not supporting the change, leaders must be quick to recognize disconnects in how employees behave and step in quickly to correct them. This is not something the change project team can do; only leaders can control the behavior of their teams.

Persist When Facing Resistance

Effective sponsors won't marginalize the change objectives to keep everyone happy. I once had a client who defined one of their core values as "respect for others." That isn't a bad thing. We all want to work in organizations where we respect one another. Unfortunately, the translation of that activity inside the organization was that you would never do anything that might make people uncomfortable. For example, over the years, the organization had become top-heavy, with multiple redundant layers of leadership in their organizational structure. It was clear that to keep the business alive and thriving, it needed to realign the global organizational structure and conduct a reduction in force. When we met with the leadership team to discuss the reductions, it was clear that the leaders were reluctant to engage in any activity that would result in a reallocation or reduction in resources. They viewed it as a violation of their core values. Unfortunately they were confusing "respect for people" with "keep everybody happy."

The reality is that most change activity is going to drive some level of temporary dissatisfaction. Avoiding driving change and/or waiting for everyone to be happy before you implement the change is a recipe for disaster.

Most changes are accompanied by some level of discomfort on the part of those who need to change, yet too often, leaders water down what they are trying to do so as not to upset employees. The question these leaders should be asking themselves is, "Do we need this change or not?" If you do, don't compromise the level of change you need to implement just to keep employees happy. At the end of the day, you'll regret not doing what needed to be done. Instead do a great job of anticipating the issues, resolving them quickly, and holding employees accountable, and you will reduce the cycle time to get to the new way of doing things. The bottom line is that if you need to change, then really change!

Fatal Flaw #2—Inability to Prioritize

Our second fatal flaw is the inability to prioritize. There are three specific leadership behaviors that lead to poor prioritization and a lack of focus: not establishing clear priorities, failing to eliminate current work to make room for new work, and changing priorities too quickly.

Establish Clear Priorities

In chapter 2, we talked about Miller's rule of seven. As a reminder, Miller's research proved that the average person is severely limited in terms of the amount of information they can receive, process, and remember. So basically Miller found that people can only remember and focus on a few things. I want to reiterate the importance of that psychological concept again. When leaders are unable to define, communicate, and manage effort toward the *most critical priorities* for the organization, effort is diluted because employees focus on what they think is important.

I once worked with a CEO who had a throw-it-all-at-the-wall-to-see-what-sticks approach to management. He absolutely refused to set clear priorities and instead felt that people should just step up to whatever he put in front of them. As a result he absolutely exhausted the organization. The chaos he caused severely damaged his reputation and the credibility of the leadership team who tried to support his approach. It drove the perception that leaders lacked empathy for the lower level employees, who had to deal with an overwhelming amount of work. His approach can work in spurts, but it is absolutely not sustainable. Leaders must define the three to five most critical priorities for the organization and then ensure ongoing focus on that work.

Decide What the Organization Must Stop Doing to Make Room for New Work

Change requires sustained energy and focus. In chapter 5 we talked about the value of conducting a work impact analysis and rebalancing the workload after a change is initiated. When asking the organization to adopt a new change (and all the work that goes with it), you can't just expect employees to absorb the new work in addition to what is currently on their plates. Stop long enough to consider what comes off the plate so that you can make space for the new work the change is going to add!

Give the Change Time to Work

Let's assume you want to take a trip to Legoland with your kids. You decide on the destination, you decide the mode of transportation, you book all the hotel stays along the way, you spend three days driving, and then once you are halfway there, you decide you're going to go to Hawaii instead. Not only have you wasted time and money getting halfway to Legoland, but the family would probably want to kick you out of the car. As silly as this example is, it is unfortunately quite common for leaders to exhibit this same behavior. I've worked with many clients who will establish a three-year plan and the associated strategic priorities and then, six months later, decide to change the priorities. Or a new leader comes into their role and decides to make their mark, so they again change priorities. Continually shifting priorities contributes to a phenomenon known as institutionalized cynicism, which causes employees to lose confidence in their leaders, distrust the organization, and become angry, dissatisfied, and disillusioned. This in turn will cause employees to just stop paying attention to what leadership says. They simply ignore messages from above and adopt an I-can-outlast-it mentality. They don't participate in the change; instead they choose to just wait until the current leader moves on and the next leader brings in his latest fad. Then they ignore that too.

Change takes time. Old habits need to die to make room for new habits, and depending on how large your organization is, it will require time for a change to be deployed at all levels of the organization. And remember, the more different the change is for those who need to change, the more energy and focus it requires. It is important to stay focused on your change objectives long enough to let the change take hold. Avoid creating a revolving door of new priorities, which will just drive organizational fatigue. Unless there is a significant reason to alter course, stick with the change long enough to allow it to work!

Fatal Flaw #3—Poor Decision-Making Practices

The third fatal flaw is an absence of good decision-making practices. Remember our discussion about Ralph earlier in this chapter? When we started the change activity, I completed an assessment of the organization, and then I met with Ralph and his executive team. I had one simple but important question for them. I asked, "Do you really have the stomach for this?"

As the change started to ramp up, it became clear that the biggest obstacle to the success of this change would be the complete lack of leadership decision-making. Planning groups would make recommendations. Good recommendations. Recommendations that were aligned with the changes that the leaders were requesting. However, the decisions that were made and agreed to in the broader groups would continually be revisited.

Not once. Not twice. But multiple times upon leaving the room. Decisions that were considered final were never final. The inability to decide, stick with that decision, and then execute it absolutely paralyzed the organization. Unfortunately it also destroyed the trust of the organization in Ralph and his leadership team. Ralph and his team failed to practice three key behaviors that would have led to more effective decision-making. This is what Ralph should have done in support of the changes he wanted.

First, *be clear on who gets to make the decision.* A lack of clarity in this area will drive redundant activity and cause conflict in the organization when multiple people feel they own the same decision. (A simple approach for clarifying decision accountability was outlined in chapter 3 when we discussed "Who has the X?")

Second, *get more comfortable making decisions in the absence of complete and exhaustive data.* The best leaders will use the eighty/twenty rule, seeking out data to inform the decisions, and then, when they have even 80 percent of the needed data, they move forward. If the decision is wrong, it'll jump up to bite you, and then you can make a different decision. But there is a cost of waiting for perfect data. You can miss market opportunities, you can lose good talent that has lost patience with your lack of disciplined decision-making, and, like Ralph, you can drive organizational fatigue because decisions are slow to come and/or are continually revisited.

Finally, *have transparency in your decision-making process.* Be clear on how decisions will be made. Will group meetings result in an agreed-upon decision? Is the group meeting just to provide input, then leaders will decide outside the room? Anything can work, but be clear about the process. When Ralph allowed his leaders to publicly commit to a final decision, it should have been final, because that was the agreed upon process. When his leaders would agree to a course of action publicly and then establish backroom deals that fundamentally altered decisions already made, it destroyed the credibility of the leadership team. Endless hours of time were wasted making group decisions that were revisited after the group meeting. If a decision is made, then do not allow backroom conversations to continually alter that decision.

Fatal Flaw #4—Ineffective Communication Practices

Our fourth fatal flaw is the inability to establish good two-way communication practices. Some changes are small and simple (for example, changing the company logo). Generally this type of change will have minimal resistance. In those cases the investment in two-way communication should be minimal. Change the logo and send out an email announcing the change. However, most changes aren't that simple, so if you think you can effectively implement significant change by just providing regular email updates, think again. Do not underestimate the criticality of good communication when implementing change.

The more I've worked with CEOs, the more I continue to understand just how lonely it is at the top. People are always telling you what you want to hear and not what you need to hear. Honestly I think that's why people in my business stay in business. Because the good ones will always tell you the truth whether you like it or not. One way to surface the truth is through data. I cannot tell you how valuable it is for a leader to hear the raw truth from employees about how they really feel about something. Colin Powell, former US secretary of state, was once quoted as saying, "The day soldiers stop bringing you their problems is the day you have stopped leading them. They have either lost confidence that you can help them or concluded that you do not care. Either case is a failure of leadership." He couldn't have been more accurate.

Most of us have had the opportunity to attend a sporting event in a large stadium. When I was in college, money was scarce, so when I had the rare opportunity to go see a game, I had to sit in the highest nosebleed seats. Several years later, when I could afford it, I would buy seats in the middle—a little more expensive but a little closer to the field. Once I had a friend offer me his seats in the end zone. I was excited because it was closer to the field, but I spent most of the time looking sideways because there was a big pole between me and the players. Later I was able to surprise my husband with first-row tickets on the fifty-yard line. We could have reached out and touched the players. All these seats offered a unique view of the field depending on where I was sitting. This concept is very applicable to change. When they run a replay on television, they provide views from multiple angles. When you lead a change, it is important to gather all the perspectives you can to fully understand what is happening on the field. You need to see the field from every angle. Where is the change working well? Why? What can you learn from where it is working well to improve it elsewhere in the organization? When employees raise concerns about the impact of the change, listen! Based on their seat in the stadium, they often see what you may fail to see from the top of the organization, so don't be defensive when they criticize the change process. Instead, listen, learn, and adapt your plan as needed. The effectiveness of your change depends on it.

Early in the change process, leaders should set the expectation that they want a structured method of gathering feedback from the field. I often use the simple survey illustrated on the next page to gather anonymous quarterly feedback from those most affected by the change. I then develop customized reports for each leader in the organization, so they receive a report card on how the change is working in their specific area. Can you distribute more complex assessments? Absolutely. But this simple format tests four essential elements of effective change: Do employees understand what you are trying to do with the change, do they feel personal accountability for getting it done, do they think leaders are supporting the change, and do they know how to escalate obstacles to success? Generally that is enough to identify issues and move forward.

Quarterly Employee Change Survey:

Four Key Success Factors	Survey Questions (Agree, Somewhat Agree, Disagree, Strongly Disagree, Don't Know)
Clarity of the Change Objectives	❑ I understand the reason for the centralized manufacturing change. ❑ This change is the right thing to do for our company.
Sense of Urgency and Personal Impact	❑ I know how I will be held accountable to support this change. ❑ I know what I need to do differently in my role as a result of the change.
Leadership Support for the Change	❑ My manager regularly communicates about the change. ❑ My manager demonstrates clear support for the change by modeling the appropriate behaviors.
Environment to Support Issue Escalation	❑ I know how to escalate issues that will impact the success of the change. ❑ I feel free to openly ask questions or express concerns related to the change.
General Input (Open-Ended)	❑ If you could offer advice to leadership about this change, what specific advice would you offer? ❑ From your perspective, what are the primary obstacles to successfully implementing this change? ❑ What suggestions do you have to overcome the obstacles?

Fatal Flaw #5—Not Recognizing When You Are Part of the Problem

The transformation project with Ralph and his team was perhaps the most challenging change (and most challenging leadership team) that I had ever worked with. I debated long and hard about how to share with them what I felt they needed to know about their own contribution to the challenges the transition team had experienced. Based on the remarkably poor behavior of the leadership team throughout the process, I wasn't confident about their ability to sustain the changes we launched. Finally, I decided to keep it simple. I captured the key elements of the five fatal flaws in the list of questions on the Five Fatal Flaws Risk Assessment shown on the following page. I ended up giving each member of the leadership team a copy. I wanted them to think more deeply about their personal role in sustaining the change. I didn't ask them to publicly share the responses; I just asked them each to add up how many yes, somewhat, or no answers they had given themselves. I then asked them to review their answers. If they were able to answer yes to most of the questions, then the likelihood that they could sustain the change was high. If most of their answers fell in the somewhat column, I told them it put them at moderate risk of not being able to sustain the change. And as you can see from Ralph's assessment, most of his answers fell in the no column, which was an indication that it was unlikely the change could sustain itself under his leadership. This exercise launched a series of discussions about the leadership changes required to sustain the change. As a result of those discussions, Ralph initiated a plan to replace himself in the organization. It was an admirable and necessary decision.

Five Fatal Flaws Risk Assessment: Ralph Jones, CEO

		Yes	Somewhat	No
Sponsorship	Do I demonstrate both public and private support for the change?	X		
	Have I provided adequate resources and appropriate funding to ensure the successful implementation of the change?		X	
	Am I visibly rewarding employees who demonstrate support for the change?			X
	Am I holding employees accountable when they do not demonstrate support for the change?			X
	Am I implementing the necessary changes, even if it causes unhappiness in the organization?			X
Clear Priorities	Have I reestablished priorities to create space for employees to execute on this change?		X	
	Am I prepared to give the change the necessary time to take hold in the organization?	X		
	Have I consciously defined what we will stop doing to make room for the new work?		X	
Decision-Making	Have I clearly defined who has decision-making authority as a result of the change?			X
	Do I demonstrate the ability to make decisions quickly, even in the absence of all the data that might be helpful?			X
	Have I ensured a transparent decision-making process to instill trust in the change process?		X	
Communication	Do I regularly communicate about the change to ensure people are aware of its importance?	X		
	Have I put in place communication practices that encourage open dialogue about the change?	X		
	Have I put in place a process that ensures employees know how to raise issues or concerns related to the change?	X		
Leadership	Do I regularly solicit feedback on what I as the leader need to do differently to implement this change?			X
	Do I accept feedback and modify my leadership approach to ensure that the change objectives are met?			X
	Total	5	4	7

Summary

So based on this chapter, here are the common pitfalls to avoid in the "C" or CHANGE PRINCIPLES component of the MOSAIC framework:

- Failing to invest the time necessary to effectively sponsor the change. (A good sponsor must be personally involved, abide by the triple constraints, ensure employees feel accountable to drive the change forward, and not marginalize what needs to be done just to keep employees happy.)

- Not setting clear priorities to ensure focus, failing to eliminate work to make room for the new work required by the change, and changing priorities too quickly. Remember that change takes time!

- Failing to make decisions with speed, without 100 percent of the data, and with a lack of transparency in how decisions are made and by whom

- Not establishing effective two-way communication practices to ensure rapid escalation of issues and obstacles to the change and failing to ensure issues can be raised with no repercussions for honest feedback from any level of the organization

- Not recognizing when you as a leader are part of the problem

The *C* in MOSAIC is unique from the other pieces. It's not really a separate tile in and of itself. The concepts outlined apply to every step of the MOSAIC framework. They are constants that must become habitual if you want your change to be effectively implemented and sustained. These five principles must become well-exercised muscles for leaders at any level. To ignore them all but guarantees failure, so ignore them at your own peril.

* * *

The Foundational Tools: Quarterly Employee Change Survey | Five Fatal Flaws Risk Assessment

Chapter 8

A Very Little Bit about Culture

If your culture supports status quo, then you will get status quo

For anyone who makes a living managing organizational change, there's a common saying we all know and understand well: "Culture eats change for lunch," or "The big fish will always eat the little fish." I believe the saying is derived from Peter Drucker, who said that "culture eats strategy for breakfast." Pick any version of the saying, but it all represents the same concept. When you are trying to implement a change, if the people who need to embrace that change don't share the beliefs and values that support the change, your change is likely to fail. It may occur as a slow backslide over a period of years, where the change is slowly abandoned as the pressure to revert to status quo deteriorates the new. Or the change is abandoned quickly as soon as the management pressure to implement the change is removed, generally replaced by something new that has piqued management's interest.

There is extensive literature on the topic of culture, so at the risk of seriously oversimplifying the topic, I'm going to keep the discussion of culture very simple and hopefully suggest some actions to help you determine the impact of culture on your ability to sustain organizational change.

I get asked all the time, "What is the ideal culture for my company?" The answer to that question is the same each time: "It depends on what your strategic business objectives are and what normative behavior you need your employees to engage in so that you can achieve those business objectives."

When I first started working with them, PAX-Z had been around for about forty-two years. In the first month of working with the leadership team, their cultural norms became very clear. There were a lot of positive things about the company, but if I had to describe the less desirable behaviors that were typical for a PAX-Z employee, I would use terms like *conflict avoidant, no sense of urgency to move quickly regardless of the negative impact on customers, decision-making that favors each business unit rather than the enterprise, laissez-faire approach to managing performance*, et cetera. Basically, if you were someone who just wanted a job where you could skate by without doing a lot of work, this was the culture for you.

When Sam came in as the new CEO, he realized he had a problem. To keep the business from continuing to decline, he needed to drive a very significant overhaul of the company. In addition to extensive operational improvements, he knew that he needed his employees to behave quite differently. He needed them to embrace and believe in values such as action orientation, the pursuit of excellence, customer-centric service, and enterprise decision-making.

In his first town hall meeting with employees, he presented his new list of desired behaviors. When it came time for questions, one of the longer-term employees stood up and said, "That's nice, but that's not what we really do around here." That one employee's statement tells you everything that you need to know about culture. Culture has nothing to do with what leaders say they want it to be; culture reflects how things really happen in the organization.

Culture is all about shared beliefs, values, and norms. What is a norm? A norm is something that could be defined as usual, typical, or standard. Leaders often think that having discussions on beliefs and values is fluffy stuff that isn't worthy of their time. This couldn't be further from the truth. Cultural change isn't about giving out banners, mugs, or T-shirts with smart slogans. Culture starts with a definition of the beliefs, values, and behaviors employees must embrace each day to accomplish strategic business objectives. Culture is the result of the actions taken and reinforced each day in terms of how leaders do the following:

- *Talk about the desired beliefs, values and expected behaviors.* Leaders need to set the stage for what typical and acceptable behavior is for the organization. Have you defined what your desired behaviors need to be to achieve your business objectives?

- *Reward the behaviors.* How are the desired behaviors continually recognized in a way that signals to the broader organization that those behaviors are valued and will be rewarded? For example, if you value growth, do you give out a quarterly growth award?

- *Reinforce the behaviors.* Does every meeting include a reminder of what 'good' looks like? Are the desired behaviors visible to employees and regularly discussed? If you see employees engage in behaviors that are counter to the desired behaviors, is it quickly corrected rather than waiting for an annual performance review?

- *Measure the behaviors.* Does your performance management process reflect a direct link between desired behaviors and feedback on how the employee does or does not display those behaviors? Including desired behaviors as part of your formal performance process gives teeth to culture change.

- *Model the behaviors they want to see in others.* As a leader, do you personally serve as a role model for others, consistently displaying the desired behaviors? We've all heard the saying "Actions speak louder than words." Leaders who preach about desired behaviors and then do the opposite have no chance of changing their culture. If you behave inappropriately, so will your employees. If you allow your leaders to behave inappropriately, so will your employees. It doesn't matter what your company brochure says about your values—employees will follow your lead.

What does culture have to do with organizational change? Well, when you are launching a change, it is important to consider what is accepted as typical behavior in the organization. It is important to evaluate if those typical behaviors support movement toward your change or away from it. Remember: culture eats change for lunch. If you are working in a culture that doesn't reinforce the behaviors you need to successfully implement your change, you will either need to change the culture or modify your change.

It can take three to five years to change the culture in an organization. This simple cultural alignment discussion tool is not the solution to changing a culture, but it provides a vehicle for the seminal conversation around what needs to change. The important thing to remember is that as you move through a change initiative, each element of the MOSAIC framework will offer an opportunity to alter the threads of the fabric that reinforce your culture, so take advantage of those opportunities as they arise.

When Sam accepted the leadership role at PAX-Z, he pulled together several of his key leaders and used the tool to evaluate how aligned the company culture was to what he wanted to accomplish. Here is the result of that discussion:

Basic Cultural Alignment Conversation

Our Existing Beliefs, Values, and Behaviors	Beliefs, Values, and Behaviors Required for Change
• Family oriented • Good work/life balance • Conflict avoidant—run from honest conversation • Siloed decision-making that favors "me," not the enterprise • Laissez-faire approach to managing performance • Backdoor decision-making is typical • Community minded • No sense of urgency to act now regardless of customer impact	• Ability to have critical conversations/open dialogue • Market-led and long-term enterprise decision-making • Performance linked to business objectives, not friendships • Transparent decision-making and moving forward once we decide • Leaders that model the way • Strong action orientation • Customer-centric in all that we do

Lever	Actions to Support and/or Realign	Owner	Due
Define	• Executive team to define the new behaviors/values for PAX-Z • Recommunicate in Q1 town hall, including link to performance review	Sam/Maggie	Oct. 1 Jan. 11
Reward	• Develop process for a "hole-in-one" award to give out quarterly at town hall • Establish the process for twenty-five-dollar "eagle awards" to be given out immediately when good behavior is observed (two per month for each leader as needed)	Doris Maggie	Dec. 22
Reinforce	• "Hole-in-one" poster in all meeting rooms • Every staff meeting starts with a callout for one employee that best modeled our culture in the prior month	Doris Executive Team & Level-Two Leaders	Feb 1 Feb 7
Measure	• Revise performance management system to reflect new behaviors/values	Maggie	Dec 22
Model	• Quarterly global survey to include feedback on management modeling the way	Doris	Mar 13

The changes that Sam was trying to implement would never survive the culture he currently had in place. There's a reason it takes a long time to change a culture. You must either replace employees who have beliefs and values that are counter to what you want the culture to be (in which case the culture can change quickly), or you must ensure that all new hires demonstrate the new beliefs and values you want in your culture (in which case the culture will change slowly over time). This is why CEOs often join an organization and quickly replace the top layer of leadership. Let's face it. It is a significant change accelerator when all the leaders have values and beliefs that are aligned with the direction the CEO is headed because you don't have leaders fighting the new way of doing things.

Unfortunately, the challenge of trying to lead a change project that is counterculture is that often the person responsible for driving the change (change project leader) isn't responsible for the overall culture of the company (CEO). PAX-Z was fortunate that Sam both understood and was willing to invest in changing his company culture. That isn't always the case. If you realize that your change is counterculture, you'll need to either pause your change effort or head down a parallel path and hope that you can work with the CEO to adjust the culture prior to the full implementation of the change. Easier said than done, but if the CEO really wants to sustain the change, they may be more open than you think to a discussion on culture.

* * *

The Foundational Tool: Basic Cultural Alignment Conversation

Chapter 9

Summary

At the conclusion of one of my most difficult transformation projects, the CEO I was working with paid me one of the best compliments of my career. We were assembled at the final celebration dinner for a three-year transformation project. When the CEO went to the podium to congratulate the organizational effectiveness team that had been working on the project, he said we reminded him of a group of nuns that he had encountered while on a long-term assignment outside the United States. He recalled that these nuns "went to the most difficult places, brought an agenda that was not their own, and stayed until the work was done." I have often reflected on that comment because I think it is an accurate way to think about this type of work.

The MOSAIC change framework provides the foundational tools (the science) to solve the most common internal organizational effectiveness and change problems, but at the end of the day, they are only tools and therefore highly dependent on the individual who chooses to use the tool. When change leaders are willing to engage in difficult conversations, take personal risks to move toward what is best for the client, and persevere when the client makes them the target of the all the frustrations that accompany transformational change? That is an art. And when the science is married with the art of organizational effectiveness, amazing things can happen in an organization.

As you work to apply the MOSAIC tools to the challenges you face in your own organization, keep in mind that the most effective change artists:

- remember that change must be managed from the perspective of the whole, not just the parts;

- know that the *what* must be defined before planning the *how*;

- only use organizational restructuring <u>after</u> ensuring role clarity and decision authority;

- recognize that having the right talent in place to execute the mission is essential;

- align the organization to ensure that the glue is in place to sustain change over time;

- bring project management discipline to the change management process; and

- have the courage to engage in the difficult conversations required to ensure adherence to key change principles.

I sincerely hope that you have found this book useful. All the foundational tools presented in this book are available for download as part of our online MOSAIC Foundations Learning Series. Once you have mastered the foundational tools, you may want to consider exploring our more advanced programs. If you would like information on our other workshops and training programs, are interested in participating in our MOSAIC online communities/forums, or are interested in becoming a MOSAIC certified change leader, you can find us at www.mosaicchange.com.

We look forward to hearing from you!

APPENDIX

The Simple MOSAIC Assessment

Organizational effectiveness and change work generally starts with some level of assessment. The assessment process helps to identify which part of the MOSAIC framework needs to be addressed. Is the mission clear, or do you have multiple departments working at cross-purposes due to a lack of strategic clarity? Do you really have to go through the pain of reorganizing your structure or just invest the time to clarify decision-making authority? Are you confident that you need to implement yet another corporate initiative, or do you need to start holding leaders accountable to implement the prior dozen that you have already launched? These are just some of the questions that should be considered before initiating a change so that you are focused on the most pressing issues for your organization.

As part of our standard change work, we conduct structured organizational assessments to quickly zero in on the key problems the client is facing. Diagnostics are usually customized based on the specific client needs and our initial client discussions. To accurately interpret the results requires some level of expertise in survey methodology; therefore we don't just want to blindly suggest a standard assessment tool. However, we have included below a short list of questions entitled "Solving the Right Problem." **This is not a full formal organizational diagnostic,** but it can provide you with a simple method to identify and then invest in solving the root-cause issues facing your organization *before* you invest money funding change efforts targeted at the wrong problem. It surfaces challenges within each component of the MOSAIC framework and provides an opportunity to include open-ended questions that can surface key themes which are specific to the organization. (The feedback on these questions will require that you invest time in a theme analysis.)

This is not an in-depth diagnostic assessment and does not measure external factors. This is intentionally designed to help you identify and resolve the most common internal issues that can prevent your organization from being able to respond most effectively to external influences. For more information on diagnostics, visit www.mosaicchange.com or consider attending our MOSAIC Assessment Fundamentals workshop.

Solving the Right Problem—The Simple MOSAIC Assessment

		Yes	Somewhat	No
Mission	The mission for our organization is clear.			
	The five most critical strategic outcomes required to achieve the mission have been defined.			
Organization	Our organizational structure effectively enables the execution of our mission.			
	Roles and responsibilities are clearly defined (e.g., employees clearly understand who is supposed to do what).			
	It is clear who has the authority to make decisions for key bodies of work.			
Staff	Our staffing strategy is linked to the strategic needs of the organization.			
	We have the needed skills and capabilities required to execute our mission.			
Alignment	Employees clearly understand the mission and key strategic outcomes and their role in executing it.			
	Employees are rewarded for work and behaviors that support the achievement of the mission.			
	The key processes required to accomplish the mission are clearly defined and efficient.			
	Our policies and practices support the achievement of the mission.			
Implementation	Our communication practices are effective.			
	We have effective practices to ensure accountability and follow-up.			
Change Principles	We have the right leaders in place to achieve our mission.			
	Our decision-making process is effective.			
	Leaders model the behaviors necessary to accomplish the mission.			
Miscellaneous	For example, "If you could only improve two things..." or "If you were CEO for the day, what two things would you fix first?"	*Requires Theme Analysis*		

For more information on diagnostic assessments, visit www.mosaicchange.com.

References

Mendelow, A. L. 1981. "Environmental Scanning: The Impact of the Stakeholder Concept." In *Proceedings from the Second International Conference on Information Systems*, 407–18. Cambridge, MA.

Miller, G. A. 1956. "The Magical Number Seven, Plus or Minus Two: Some Limits on Our Capacity for Processing Information." *Psychological Review* 63, no. 2: 81–97. https://doi.org/10.1037/h0043158.

Project Management Institute. 2004. *A Guide to the Project Management Body of Knowledge (PMBOK Guide)*, 3rd ed. Newtown Square, PA: Project Management Institute.